Sacramental Cocoa

Sacramental Cocoa

And Other Stories
from the Parish of the Poor

Lynn E. Perry

Westminster John Knox Press
Louisville, Kentucky

Scripture quotations from the Revised Standard Version of the Bible are copyright 1946, 1952, © 1971, 1973 by the Division of Christian Education of the National Council of the Churches of Christ in the U.S.A. and are used by permission.

Grateful appeciation is extended to the Jenkins Family Partnership for permission to use lyrics from "The Caretaker," by Gordon Jenkins.

Book design by Drew Stevens
Cover design by Tanya R. Hahn

First edition

Published by Westminster John Knox Press
Louisville, Kentucky

This book is printed on acid-free paper that meets the American National Standards Institute Z39.48 standard. ∞

PRINTED IN THE UNITED STATES OF AMERICA

95 96 97 98 99 00 01 02 03 04 — 10 9 8 7 6 5 4 3 2 1

Library of Congress Cataloging-in-Publication Data

Perry, Lynn E.
    Sacramental cocoa and other stories from the parish of the poor / Lynn E. Perry. — 1st ed.
        p.   cm.
    ISBN 0-664-25521-3 (alk. paper)
    1. Church work with the poor—Illinois—Chicago. 2. Uptown Ministry (Chicago, Ill.) 3. Chicago (Ill.)—Church history—20th century. I. Title.
BR560.C4P47   1995
277.73′110829—dc20   94-43406

Love to Scott,
who has always encouraged me in all things,
and to our children,
Amy, Bonnie, and Andrew,
who have always loved stories

Contents

Acknowledgments

$\mathcal{S}$ome names and events in this book have been changed or represent composite people or situations, to protect privacy.

I owe special thanks to staff and coworkers who dedicated themselves unselfishly to be God's servants in this special place and have consented to be included by name: the Rev. Edgar M. (Mick) Roschke, the Rev. Thomas Tews, Ruth S. Forni, Janet N. Steinbauer, Andrea (Ann) Schultz Arnold, Sister Mary Kay Flanigan, the Rev. James F. Hennig, Richard W. Grooms, Martha J. Grooms, the Rev. Marianka Fousek, Jackie Raino, Dorothy Martin Murphy, Elizabeth Hernandez Alamo, the Rev. Larry Morkert, Roberta Ulrich-de Oliveira, and Arne Buehler.

Appreciation and thanks are due to people in the stories who have agreed to appear as themselves: Floyd Hansen, Violet Carroll, Richard Walker, Emil Felcan, Reba Dickson, Joseph Polk, Jeannie Arndt, Patricia M. Barger, and Diane M. Yost.

I would like to acknowledge with gratitude those who read the manuscript and encouraged me to pursue publication: R. Ronald Holland, Mina C. Jewett, J. Barrie Shepherd, Carolyn and David Utech, James Hayford, Debra L. Rice, Lois M. Barrows, and Frederick W. Reklau.

Introduction

*W*hat's a WASP like you doin' here?" their suspicious eyes would say, while their mouths tried to control a smirk. They had a right to ask the question. Indeed, what did a white, Anglo-Saxon Protestant, suburban housewife have in common with an inner-city collection of poor people of various races, who bore the burdens of the underclass—hunger, disease, addictions, violence, unemployment, illiteracy, and despair? Nothing—and everything!

The plight of the poor was brought to my attention in a unique way by two young clergymen, Mick Roschke and Tom Tews. They visited our congregation, Grace Lutheran Church in Evanston, to describe their ministry to the people in the Uptown section of Chicago's North Side.

Uptown was a ten-block by ten-block area wedged between the Gold Coast wealth along Marine Drive, adjacent to Lake Michigan's Lake Shore Drive on the east and Western Avenue on the west. Uptown was twenty minutes north of Chicago's Loop, with Foster and Montrose Avenues the north and south boundaries. The landmarks of Uptown's golden days were near—the Aragon Ballroom, where all the bands of the Big Band era played; the Edgewater Beach Hotel, where the wealthy vacationers played; and the Graceland Cemetery, where local citizens, noteworthy politicians and philanthropists, movie stars, and Chicago gangsters were buried—when the playing ceased.

As the process of gentrification went on in the city, the exorbitant costs of rent forced the poor into Uptown. With rising rents, businesses relocated in distant suburbs, and the working poor without cars were stranded and could no longer get to their jobs. There was no public transportation to the distant locations, so those able to work had to rely on the day-labor agencies or, as they were referred to on the street, "the slave market."

Our congregation's response to Mick and Tom's presentation was a pledge of monthly financial aid, plus the promise that occasional collections of food would be delivered to the storefront location where "The Ministry," as the pastors called it, was located.

I had previously felt a tug to respond to needs beyond those of my family, but had no idea what I could do. I had also been hesitant because I wanted to be with my young children. Then Pat Barger, my friend and neighbor and also the director of the Loyola Child Guidance Clinic, invited me to lead a little play group called the Sibling Group for Language Stimulation. The children were siblings of psychotic children and needed language enhancement. My own children, preschoolers at that time, were the normal children who would be models. One morning a week we all went to Loyola University for the little play group. That experience prompted me to organize a similar play group at our church and led naturally to my volunteering to lead a play group for children in Uptown.

Jan Steinbauer and Ruth Forni were newly graduated teachers who also had felt called to work with the children of this area. They developed a program for educational enrichment for the children and called it the Learning Center, which became an evolving but constant offering at The Ministry. With Mick and Tom, Jan and Ruth made up the staff at that time. When I volunteered to work with a preschool group, they invited me to come to talk with them about it. After our discussion, they arranged with the mothers of their learning center children for a group of preschool children to come to a play group.

The exit from the elevated train at Lawrence Avenue led me into another world. I wasn't sure that I was prepared for it. It looked different; it smelled different; it sounded different. The elevated line itself was familiar, with stops at Children's Memorial Hospital and the Lincoln Park Zoo, and doors that opened directly into Marshall Field's. This, however, was the first time that I had ever gotten off at Lawrence Avenue.

It was February of 1974. The seasonal crisp cold and snow was interrupted by a gray, drizzly, and raw day. The revolving door from the stairway at the station led to the newsstand and the sidewalk on Lawrence Avenue. The smell of thawing ice on the cement in a poor neighborhood is nauseating. The dirt in the cracks smells different from the dirt on lawns. The station is damp and reeks of urine, tobacco, and the fading vapor from empty wine bottles couched in brown paper bags. Intended as a disguise, the bag also keeps a person's hand from freezing to the neck of the bottle when the temperature drops. Street people seldom wear gloves. The slush the day I arrived was mixed with mud and the smell of wet paper. The sounds of traffic, the elevated train, and frequent sirens were indicators that here was a concentrated population. Accents overheard were varied and pronounced—country, Southern black, Mexican, Puerto Rican, varied Native American, Middle Eastern. The standard midwestern English of the newscaster was rare.

When I entered on my first day, I expected as many as twenty-five children. With a guitar case in one hand and a canvas bag with toys, puzzles, and treats in the other, I was ready. At least, that's what I thought. But nobody showed up! *Nobody!* The teachers were embarrassed. Lesson one for me—about different kinds of poor people. Some were not just people without money, but were people without hope, motivation, education, or a sense of responsibility. Such characteristics would keep some people poor forever. I scooped up my gear and headed out to one family's apartment—I would bring preschool to the home.

In 1975, the four staff people plus the community volunteer staff were increasingly busy. Worship, Bible study classes, after-school learning center and tutoring, food pantry, clothing room, and outreach programs to supporting congregations were all in full swing, and there was need for a receptionist. The staff interviewed and hired me for the job, and Jan took over and expanded the preschool program.

My job changed in three weeks when I began to interview the people who came for food. I worked hard to discover and try to meet the needs of the people who came to my office—home visits in addition to food, bedding, and clothes, if necessary, hospital visits, advocacy with the public agencies, and so on. When, in one week, two of the poorest elderly people brought me candy bars because they knew I liked chocolate, I knew God was teaching me things about generosity and community and love that were changing how I thought and who I was.

Change also affected the makeup of our staff dramatically in 1979 when Reverend Mick, Reverend Tom, and Ruth each left for new ministries elsewhere. Milt Smith and Martha Grooms, who had begun as volunteers like me, had joined the staff years before. The Rev. Jim Hennig had moved from board member to staff member. Ann Schultz, a Lutheran deaconess, and Sister Mary Kay Flanigan, a Franciscan sister with a degree in social work, were hired, and we all breathed a sigh of relief. In my years at The Ministry, additional staff included Richard Grooms, Roberta Ulrich, Dorothy Martin, Liz Hernandez, the Rev. Larry Morkert, the Rev. Marianka Fousek, and Arne Buehler. What it meant to work together as a team was demonstrated to me at a staff Christmas party one year when I realized that nine of us were standing in my kitchen, each intent on a task—peeling potatoes, washing lettuce, and such—and we were not getting in one another's way.

Hundreds of people, hundreds of conversations, and hundreds of pictures come to mind when I think of The Ministry. One year I was working on a banner for Palm Sunday—a giant banner with leaves and letters spelling out "Hosanna." I had left it on a table in the main room downstairs. When I looked over the banister the next morning, I saw that not only was the room crammed tightly with more than thirty people waiting for food but half a dozen folks had gathered up chairs around the table and were carefully stitching green leaves and red letters onto the immaculate white cloth. They included an Hispanic woman who spoke no English, a young man who was a mental patient, two elderly women—one Jewish, one black—and young mothers from the preschool program—one blond and one black. One of the pastors on our board came by for a meeting, but first he too sat down to stitch. We were giving out food upstairs, and they were feeding the soul downstairs. Giving and receiving, and receiving and giving—the lines were a bit blurry.

It became increasingly clear to me that the person who benefited the most from my work was Lynn Perry. Once I recognized that, there was never again a question about why I was there. I went there because I truly felt called to be there and knew that it was a good thing to do. I did do good things—I believed that then and believe it now—but I was also the one who learned, who received, who was accepted, who was loved. The reason I was there was to experience that so I could tell others.

Many times I felt in over my head. I wished I had the training and education of the professional staff at The Ministry—the clergy, the teachers, social worker, business manager, deaconesses. Even the staff people from the community had the de facto credibility of street education. I would sit knee to knee listening to someone describe a situation alien to my lifestyle and think, What am I doing here? What right do I have to hold this person's offering of pain, or confession, or faith, or a chocolate bar? I would be riveted to my chair in prayer, asking God to be in my mind, to give me the words the person needed at the moment. Then I would focus on the person and ask the same thing—to let me see the spirit of God in the person. As I was led deeper and deeper into a prayer life, the words of Jesus to Paul became the words of Jesus to me also: "My grace is sufficient for you, for my power is made perfect in weakness" (2 Cor. 12:9).

There is a point in any deep relationship when people stop keeping score. One no longer says, "It's my turn to invite them to dinner," or "I owe her a favor because she did . . ." or "I need to write him because he called last week." There was a point in my nine years there that the line was crossed and there were no more tallies. We were together. We worshiped together; we prayed together; we cared for one another when one got sick; we celebrated birthdays and weddings and baptisms and funerals. We had meals together— beer and pizza, cake and coffee, sandwiches and milk, tea and sympathy, bread and wine. And always, the lines were a little fuzzy about who was in ministry to whom.

Ultimately, what we had in common were love and concern for our families, loyalty to our friends, affection for our pets, devotion to one another, and sometimes a passion for chocolate. The quintessential bond, though, was our response to God, and that transcended our differences in every other aspect.

These stories are about people. They are about people when the scorekeeping stopped and the relationship began. These are stories about ministry. This is not, however, a handbook on social ministry, though there are things to learn here about that topic. This is really a love story. These people crowded my head and my mind until I could think of nothing else. It seemed important to write about them so others could love them too.

Sacramental Cocoa

Sacramental Cocoa

The process was quite simple, really. The Ministry, a church-supported place of caring for the poor in the Uptown section of Chicago, included a food pantry. I was one of the staff people who interviewed those who came for food. We asked some very routine and basic questions: name, address, date of birth, number of people in the household, source of income. In the nine years that I was at The Ministry, this simple process brought thousands of people through the door, but not one of them had a simple story.

There were many reasons that a person could run out of food. The answers to our simple questions might later lead to more sensitive questions requiring follow-up, care, intervention, or referral: What's your new address since your previous building burned? You have a nasty black eye—Do you need to talk about that? If someone had been robbed, we would provide comfort and information about procedures for filling out police reports. If a person needed to buy medication not covered by Medicaid, the doctor could usually prescribe something else that did qualify. If an alcoholic spouse was using the family's limited income to buy beer, Al-Anon could help. If there had been a fire, a very common occurrence in Uptown, blankets and household items were provided.

The interview was not a third degree, but a way to discover needs behind needs, to care for people in a wider variety of ways.

In my second week of interviewing I met Margaret. Margaret was a very slim, tiny lady, elderly and a bit stooped. She kept her head cocked like a sparrow inspecting a sidewalk tidbit. Her shy, angled look was augmented by her odd-shaped jaw. Margaret had had surgery for cancer, resulting in the removal of a large portion of her left jaw. The concavity caused by this surgery gave her face its look of appealing inquisitiveness.

2 · *Sacramental Cocoa*

Margaret's missing jaw also meant that forming words was a laborious process for her, with mixed results. Understanding Margaret was very difficult, but it was important not to embarrass her by asking her to repeat herself a dozen times. With total concentration and a healthy imagination, I was able to catch about half of what she said. It came down to three essentials: She was awaiting a space in a public housing building; she liked tomato soup; she adored cocoa.

With limited food supplies available, we had a hard-and-fast rule: after the established number of people had been served and we had to turn people away, other staff people were not supposed to give food to later walk-ins. Everyone broke the rule. We argued about this at every staff meeting. Still, everyone on the staff broke the rule. Each of us had special "sheep," and there were times when we just could not say no. I broke the rule for Margaret. The rationalization came easily for me with her. After all, she just wanted a box of cocoa!

Margaret appeared once or twice a month from May until the following April. She came in one day so excited it was almost impossible for me to understand her. When she had settled down, she was able to explain there was finally an apartment available in a senior citizen housing project on Chicago's West Side.

She was thrilled, and we were delighted for her. We helped her make plans for her move, knowing it meant we would not be seeing her anymore because she would be so far away. She had all kinds of things—chairs, a table, dishes, small household items—everything she needed but a decent mattress. We knew that we could find that and asked her to call when she got settled. Meanwhile, we scrounged around. The office had many calls from people who were moving or buying new things and were eager to donate all kinds of items. Sure enough, we located a mattress and arranged with Margaret for a day and time to deliver it.

My mind was full of the busy, overscheduled day ahead of me when we got ready to go to Margaret's, and I knew that Reverend Tom, who was driving, also had a full schedule. Tom drove his old blue heap—actually half blue and half rust—a standard transmission car that always ran. With the mattress tied precariously to the top, where it had been hoisted by several burly volunteers in front of our building, we set off on the thirty-minute ride through midday traffic on our way to Margaret's new home.

There was something about Tom that brought out the buried zaniness in me. As time-pressured as we were, the ride was fun, with my holding on to the mattress through the window on the passenger side and Tom's swerving and turning as if we were in a silent movie being chased by the Keystone Kops. Many times we almost lost the mattress. It was a relief to arrive and realize we had made it—certainly we had outrun our phantom pursuers!

I went into the building's entryway to buzz Margaret to let her know we had arrived. When I went back to the car, there was Tom looking glumly at the mattress. It was big! We both realized we had no idea how to get this mattress up to Margaret's new home. It was not in a box. It did not have side grips. There it loomed, like a weeping meringue, drooping slightly to one side of Tom's car as it had drooped for the whole, hair-raising journey.

We pulled and it slipped. We pushed and it slid. Then we slid. About this time Margaret arrived at the front door with the custodian from her building and a neighbor in tow. With that much muscle available to her, we were able to consider the delivery complete. We could head back to our afternoonful of things to do.

Except that Margaret asked if we couldn't stop in for a minute.

Crunch! There are times in my life when I look back with utter amazement to find that I have been miraculously rescued from myself. There are times when, if I had gone about doing what I was doing, I would have missed what I was called to do at that time—and never even have known it.

This was one of those times. I knew Tom had a busy afternoon. He knew that I had a busy afternoon. A quick glance to each other, though, confirmed that we should accept Margaret's invitation, so shyly given. Up the elevator to the eleventh floor, in the door behind the men and the mattress we went. A sweet, immaculate, bright apartment it was, and in front of a large picture window overlooking the city, a tiny table, with delicate pink-and-white dishes, was set for three—with cookies and cocoa.

We were sober going home. No horsing around, no zaniness, but a lot of thankfulness. We were thankful that our leashes had been snapped to attention. We had heard Margaret. Something in her voice, her so-hard-to-understand words, had hit us just right, so that we accepted her invitation. We received her holy, sacrificial offering to us—the sacramental cocoa.

John

John was always around. I don't remember being introduced to him or not knowing who he was. Although he tended to remain in the background, he was well known to the staff as a person who just dropped in and as a person who came in need. He was there for every reason and for no reason. I liked him very much, and it was almost impossible to have a conversation with him without getting into an argument.

John reminded me somewhat of Robert Mitchum, except that John's face was a bit broader, his smile wider, and he was more baritone than bass. He was tall, had straight gray hair parted on the side, brown eyes, a few freckles, and a very crooked nose caused by a long history of trouble. I think of John as sort of blue and gray. He wore blue trousers and a gray jacket, or gray trousers and a blue windbreaker, gray shirt and gray pants, black shoes. He never wore jeans; he never wore sneakers. His clothes rarely fit—everything was from a church clothing rack, ours or someone else's— but blue and gray were the colors.

Everyone knew John. He'd been in Uptown many, many years. He had worked out of the day-labor agencies—the so-called slave market—in his younger, healthier years. He drank in all the bars, staggered across all the street corners, and haunted every food pantry, detox center, and meal site. I don't recall ever seeing him with anyone. He moved along with a crowd, without seeming part of it. He was alone in a group, solitary in his surroundings, singular in a plurality.

John had a wonderful smile—sunshine from deep inside seemed to radiate from him, but he also had a quick temper and could be fiercely angry with the same totality as he could be sunny. Courtly mannered, with some shy ways, he did not track very well in conversation. He seemed to be missing some basic comprehension skills. John had a fraternal twin named Jane who was a medical technician. John had the looks; Jane had the brains.

In the early years at The Ministry we operated at street level in a storefront building. In its youth the building had belonged to a furrier. There was a heavy, vault-type door in the rear that led to the cellar and what was once a fur storage space. The learning center was in the basement, but all offices and counseling services were at street level. People would congregate in the front waiting area on food mornings and would often drop in during the afternoon to have a cup of coffee or to sit in the large back-room open area and read the newspaper. The offices were off the corridor that ran between the small front area and the large back area, so staff were visible and readily available. John was around often, for food or not for food, for worship or coffee—a fixture.

I had talked with John some during food interviews. He had grown up in Morton Grove, a suburb of Chicago, and attended parochial school there until he was sixteen. He'd joined the armed services then, returning to the suburbs when his hitch was up. He described his family and many siblings, especially his twin, the games he'd played as a child, and the ordeal of dating. He had not had a particularly happy adolescence. John had met his wife at a dance. His descriptions of her were drawn with anger and bitterness. She was pregnant when he married her, and John had felt trapped by that. They had had three children, two boys and a girl, and his wife had grown fat and contemptuous of him. They both drank heavily, and their life together assumed the characteristics of one long drunken brawl, punctuated by episodic employment and a meal here and there. She had a lover, he discovered. John described the man as a crazy Russian who drank vodka. Though John was a notoriously unreliable reporter, in his version the finale involved his being punched, then pushed through a glass door. John lay in wait for "that crazy damn Russian," then beat his head in, hid the body behind some bushes, and headed north to Canada, where he worked as a logger for about ten years. At least, that's what he told me.

He returned to Chicago, saw his kids on very rare occasions, grieved for a love he had never had but craved, and for a time worked day labor. He was in his mid-forties when I met him. At this point he rarely worked, but hung out on the street.

One day in January of 1976, I was walking down the street when I spotted John. He hadn't been around for about two months, and seeing him made me realize that I had missed him. I hailed him, caught up with him, and matched his stride. "Where have you been, John? We have all missed you."

He gave me a secretly knowing, sidelong glance and a sort of huffy snort, and said, "Why, Mrs. Perry, I knew you were mad at me, and figured I wasn't welcome anymore."

I stopped, startled, amid sidewalk traffic, and turned to face him wide-eyed. "John, what on earth are you talking about?"

With badgering from me, he finally told this story: He'd been in his apartment napping when I had knocked on the door. He had invited me in. He described what I was wearing and how cold I looked, and said he had asked me if I'd like a cup of tea. While he was fixing a cup of tea for me, another staff person had broken down the door and accused John of molesting me, so he knew that I was mad and had stayed away.

Words did not come. My shoes were cemented to the sidewalk. "John, that did not happen," I finally said quietly. He was furious and began to yell, creating a minor scene on Sheridan Road, asking if I was calling him a liar and screaming that he was telling the truth.

"I don't think you're lying," I tried to reassure him, "but you might have had a nightmare. I haven't been to your apartment, no one from the office has broken in any doors, and none of us are mad at you." I looked at what he was wearing. Blue trousers and a girl's white blouse for a shirt, with sleeves halfway to his elbows and shoulder seams halfway to his neck, even though it was January.

"John, please come back to the office with me. You'll see that no one is mad at you, and besides, you need a shirt. This is a girl's blouse and it doesn't fit you—it's too small."

He looked a bit dazed and distracted. "Oh, yeah, I guess that's why it feels so uncomfortable," he said, tugging at the sides of the shirt and trying to make it reach his waist. He wouldn't accompany me, though—said that he had things to do. So I asked him to promise that he would come by soon. He needed to get some clothes, and everyone would want to see him. He nodded agreement, and some of his anger seemed to have subsided. We parted company at the corner of Lawrence Avenue as I headed for the B train and he headed for supper at the Salvation Army.

John's behavior exemplified for me that of many desocialized people: they had an enormous need for relationship, but the smallest encounter could be misunderstood. Care and compassion for John had to be demonstrated in a very clear-cut way, so that he could not interpret any action as flirtatious or seductive. People like John were so lonely it would be easy to take emotional advantage of them, and to do so would be a horrible cruelty. I would have to keep on my toes to be John's friend.

Julie

When I first met Julie, in May of 1975, she was about eight months pregnant with her sixth child. She was well known to The Ministry and, as I was to discover over the years, well known to practically every agency in the city. Everyone in Uptown knew her. She intertwined herself more and more in my life as the years went by.

Julie gave birth to a daughter in June and named her Jill. Of her first three children, two she had given away and a third was taken by the state. After the first three children, Julie had Terence. Following Terence was Emily, and then Jill, her sixth child.

Julie was about five feet three inches tall, with narrow shoulders and very wide hips. She weighed more than two hundred pounds, and she wore T-shirts and polyester slacks and oxfords with no socks. She was the ugliest woman I ever saw—so ugly that she was almost cute. She had long dark hair that hung in straight, matted strings, a sallow complexion, small dark eyes with heavy brows, a long scoop of a nose, big ears, and a lower jaw that extended far beyond her upper jaw, which sat in the lower jaw the way a bird nestles in a nest. She had no teeth.

Her real name, she confided, was Julietta. Her son Terence was black. He was handsome, with enormous chocolate eyes in a smiling chocolate-pudding face. Julie had given birth to him in a motel someplace in the city. She didn't know who the father was—didn't even know his name. Once she told me, "And if I ever get my hands on him, I'll kill him!"

Emily was the most beautiful little girl I had ever seen. I would look at her, look at Julie, look back at Emily, and recall a biology text on genetics that described how traits can be passed along for many generations before they surface, so characteristics that would not seem to come from a child's parents appear as if from nowhere.

Emily had curly blond hair and clear blue eyes and appeared to be a happy, smiley child.

There were concerns about Emily, because up to the time of the birth of the new baby, Emily had not yet walked, though she was sixteen months old. A caseworker from the Illinois Children's Home and Aid Society (ICH&A) had been keeping an eye on Julie and her doings. As it turned out, Emily had spent her life in the stroller; there was no crib. She had never been given the opportunity to crawl around or to walk. As soon as that need was recognized and addressed, Emily walked quickly and made strides in language as well.

When Julie would arrive for food, Terence, three, was walking at her side. The baby was lying in the stroller and Emily was sitting on one side of the stroller. As beautiful as Emily was, she was always filthy. She rarely wore diapers, nor did the baby, for that matter. They usually were diapered in a towel of some sort. Julie herself was rather dirty—her hands and fingernails were layered in dirt, her face might have jelly or juice on it, and her slacks were streaked with urine.

Julie lived with a series of men. One was Wallace, a generation older and an alcoholic. When he wasn't drinking, he kept house, did the cooking, and cared for the children. When drunk, he'd beat Julie and Terence, and she would move in with Jeff.

Jeff was the biological father of Emily (though years later he said he wasn't so sure anymore), and when sober not at all a bad sort of guy. Jeff was an alcoholic too. When he was not drinking he would work, but when he was drinking, he also was violent with Julie and the children, beating Terence and burning Emily with cigarettes. Then Julie would go back to Wallace. During one of these interludes she moved in with a fellow named Carlo. Carlo was swarthy and sweaty-looking, and probably did drugs.

Julie never had any money, not even right after receiving her welfare check. Her day began early, and in all the years I knew her, no matter where she lived, from 4000 north to 5200 north, she was always on the street by six o'clock in the morning to go to the Salvation Army at Sunnyside and Broadway, 4600 north, for breakfast with the children. It could be a hundred degrees in the shade and Julie was on the street. It could be twenty below, with howling

Chicago winds, and Julie was trudging along with the children. From the Salvation Army she would come to our building, or if she had received her limit of food for the month from us, she would go to St. Thomas of Canterbury's food pantry.

She rarely had an apartment to herself; rather, she lived with one of the men in her round-robin of acquaintances. When her welfare check arrived on the third of every month, she would buy a bag of groceries, and her current gentleman friend would pocket the rest. She also gave money away.

Each staff person took several turns at trying to get Julie to understand how to behave responsibly with her money and her food stamps, and to warn her of the implications regarding her children. She was always very agreeable, and it was impossible to tell if she really didn't understand or was simply incapable of standing up to the present boyfriend. She had a patter of words that were strung together almost like memorized speeches or portions of dialogue that she had heard somewhere. Talking to her was like talking to an automaton. And here was this new baby, Jill. I never did know who the father was, and I don't know if Julie did. She was an odd baby—she didn't make much noise, she was long and pale, and she just sort of lay there.

Julie's caseworker at ICH&A would call to check on Julie's progress, or I would call him to badger him to do something. In late October of 1975 the baby was admitted to Children's Memorial Hospital and listed as FTT, or failure to thrive. Failure to thrive is a measurable syndrome. A child who does not grow and develop within any of the standard guidelines is observed and, in this case, hospitalized.

Our son Andrew was in Children's Memorial Hospital at the same time. Andrew was eight, and we had been waiting since he was born for a heart catheterization. Eight was the optimum age, we had been told, and Andrew had been healthy enough to postpone the procedure until then. As I was in the hospital, I went up to the nursery to peek in at Julie's baby girl. She was in a large baby ward, with cribs in a circle around the room. There were only about three other babies there, and they were sick but normal, lively, gurgling and cooing babies. Jill was different. She just lay there. There were mobiles and toys above and around the crib, but she just stared. She didn't move much—didn't wave her arms or examine her toes or coo or do anything. She just lay there.

Jill was never returned to Julie. She remained in the hospital for another two weeks and then was placed in a preadoptive home. Julie spoke to me about her from time to time in sentences that began, "When I get Jill back . . . ," but I think she was relieved to have her gone. She had one hand for Terence and one for Emily, and that was about all she could manage. I began the long process of keeping careful documentation on Julie, Emily, and Terence. I had an idea that it would be necessary.

Ray

We on the staff of The Ministry were frequently approached by guilt-ridden church people who would grasp our hands and gush over our sanctity in hushed and breathless tones. We each knew secretly, though, that while the work might be tiring and require lots of physical energy, plus the energy to deal with the frustration of trying to puzzle out the impossible, we were really the ones getting the goodies. There was never any doubt in my mind, and each staff person always said the same thing: "We are the ones who benefit from this work."

It's difficult to keep something like that from sounding goody-goody. I remember one volunteer, Jeannie, who came into the office after having scoured a truly filthy hovel, and then said, "You people are just marvelous. I don't know how you do it!" Yet she was the one who had done it! All that the office staff did was put a volunteer on the track of something that had to be done.

My heart was with our volunteers and supporters, though, because I had started at The Ministry as a guilt-ridden suburbanite and could recognize the unspoken plea: Isn't there something I can do? Do you have any use for me? I want to help. I don't want to be a "them" forever, but I don't know what to do. I struggled with the question of what to do for several years, during which the only answer I was given was to help serve coffee at the coffee hour at church.

The person who set me on the path away from guilt was a lean and lanky guy named Ray. Ray was very tall and very skinny. The skinny was from a lifetime of booze and pills without food. He was also a perpetual-motion person—he sat but was never still. He had light brown, wispy hair, wavy and thinning, and it hung just below the ears. He had blue eyes and a Fu Manchu mustache, and he laughed easily. He wore bell-bottom blue jeans, leather vests and flowered shirts, chains, boots, and a big watch with a leather band. I called him Uncle Ray. Ray was one of Reverend Mick's "grace for the moment" people. We had a lot of those. Many of our people went in and out of sobriety, in and out of bouts of debilitating mental illness, in and out of hospitals or institutions. For one year Ray crossed the tracks and lived like a whole person. In that year he was clean—off drugs and alcohol. He attended AA meetings and encouraged many others to join a group. He showered regularly, paid his rent, and ate three squares a day by means of the salary he earned as part of the paid staff. Ray had everything going for him—for twelve months, one year. Then came an anniversary. The problem with anniversaries of troublesome things is that sometimes, to prove that one has mastered the demon, one tries to demonstrate mastery of the demon. That was the beginning of the end for Ray.

He began to slip. He had a couple of slips. Then he took some money from the safe. Then he began to miss work. He got behind in his rent. He moved in with a buddy—a big mistake. He tried jobs out of the "slave market." He got injured and needed hospitalization. The injury caused headaches. That frightened Ray, and he upped his habit a bit.

Life ended for Ray in an alley. In hindsight, though, I remember few details of the slide because I learned so well the lesson when Ray was straight, his "grace for the moment" year.

My first day of work on the staff was May 19, and my role for the first two weeks was to answer the phone, pull files, pour coffee—general receptionist duties. It was pleasant and chaotic. I saw everything that was going on and met all the people on the street, in a total-immersion experience. After two weeks, Reverend Mick decided that with someone at the desk all the time he could spend more time doing home visiting, so my job changed: I would now do the food interviewing along with Reverend Tom and Ray. Tom gave me the training for the interviewing; Ray taught me about the street.

The English District Convention for the Lutheran Church was being held at the end of June, and both pastors, Mick and Tom, and both teachers, Ruth and Jan, would be going. "I guess we should close that day—there won't be anyone here to do the food," Mick said. I told him I thought that we could stay open, and Ray and I could handle the interviews. Milt Smith, whom we called Smitty, was downstairs bagging the groceries—we'd do okay. Mick looked a bit downcast and said there really was not enough food.

The guilt-ridden suburban housewife emerged from the employee, and withdrawing my weapon, a grocery store check-cashing card, I said, "I'll buy the groceries." Ray and I went to the nearest grocery chain store and shopped. I bought fifteen boxes of cereal, fifteen jars of peanut butter, fifteen cans of tuna fish, fifteen cans of vegetables, fruit, and juice, fifteen boxes of spaghetti, cans of soup, and boxes of powdered milk. Feeling definitely self-satisfied, I helped Ray put the stuff on the shelves in the pantry to be ready for our food day, and went home.

Ray met me at the door in the morning when my key was still in the lock. "Lynn, I need to talk to you," he whispered. He was not happy. He put his arm on my shoulder and steered me around the front desk and the people in line for groceries, into his office. He indicated a chair and I sat down. He looked pained, embarrassed. He looked like someone who just did not know how to begin, and after saying as much, he continued, "I hate to tell you this, but the food is gone. The food you bought yesterday is gone."

"All of it?" I asked.

"Well, no, but most of it."

He wanted to do something—make it right, make me feel okay, bash somebody—but I shook my head, closed my eyes, and fanned my fingers at him for a moment. Some things inside me began to shift and flow into a new spot. Something clicked. I looked up at Ray and felt very relaxed. "It's okay, Ray. It was a good lesson, an important lesson. Don't worry about it. Let's go take a look at what we have. We'll work with that. When it's gone, it's gone. That's all we can do."

We went downstairs, and I discovered that Ray's idea of all gone and mine were a bit different. There certainly was a big dent in the supplies, but the pantry wasn't completely empty. There was some stuff there, and Smitty could just spread it around. We'd see how many were here for food and go from there.

Of all the things that people taught me—and there was much, for each one taught something over the nine years—the lesson of that day, the first month on the job, affected more than any my whole attitude about being in Uptown and working with the poor. The sense of guilt that hovered around me because I lived in a house and had a bed and food and, by standards of the world, an affluent life, would have crippled me and made me pity the poor. I had unconsciously taken on this guilt for my neighbors also. All the members of my church, my family, and my friends—they were added for good measure. My conclusion was that if someone had something, it was at the expense of someone else. The haves must be cheats who padded expense accounts, cheated on income taxes, and were the oppressors. The poor were the victims. This was not something I had articulated at the conscious level; it was just a hidden assumption that was in my head, one whose existence I hadn't even realized until the food was stolen.

In those quiet moments while I sat in the chair in Ray's office, the feeling that I was experiencing was relief. I was relieved that I could feel something besides pity. Yes, the poor were victims of oppression, but they were also victims of one another. Maybe some of my neighbors, friends, and fellow parishioners were cheats; but they also staffed the hospital, library, and music programs as volunteers, served on boards of this and that, and gave their 10 percent off the top. There were good and bad among the rich. There were good and bad among the poor. And there was good and bad in me.

Lorraine and Martha

*M*artha was a volunteer for The Ministry, and she had been helping with the distribution of clothing for about a year before I began to volunteer. When I was the preschool volunteer, Martha's two youngest children were in my group. When I became an employee for The Ministry I no longer did the preschool, but I still saw Martha for a "howdy" now and then. Within a year, Martha became a part-time staff person also, and we began to fall into step with each other more often.

The way you see people changes as you know them, and twenty-two months after meeting Martha, I saw her. It was the Fourth Sunday of Advent, and for me it would be a twelve-hour workday. On this day would be the gift exchange for The Ministry worshiping community, learning center children, and food people.

Tabor Lutheran Church was hosting a Christmas party that would begin with worship. First came the ferrying of all those who wished to attend. A local church, Pilgrim Lutheran Church, had a day school, which meant they had a school bus to lend us to pick up our people. Then each staff person drove a carload, until everyone who wanted to participate had been transported. Martha rode with me to give me directions on the one-way streets and to help load the gifts into the station wagon. Then we picked up Lorraine and her three children. For weeks our city and suburban supporters had been bringing gifts for the poor, and these would be distributed at the celebration following worship.

My home was about forty-five minutes away, so I'd been up and out at the crack of dawn, leaving my own family to the mercy of parishioners for transportation to church and Sunday school. We'd join up later in the afternoon.

As Martha rode in the navigator position and Lorraine in the middle, these two women educated me about their lives, hard times, and an eternal hopefulness that some are blessed with. Lorraine was from rural Maine, and she had an older brother. While her father, whom she adored, was away in the service during World War II, her mother did not keep the home fires burning, and when her father returned, her parents were divorced. Her mother moved to Chicago, and Lorraine and her brother remained with her dad. She spoke of occasional summer visits to her mother, and told how, when her mother was too drunk to cook, she had learned to cook at six years of age, standing on a kitchen chair because she was too small to reach the stove. Her mother had remarried and had several small children, and Lorraine was taking care of everyone.

Life in Maine with her dad was normal until he married a pretty young woman who was nineteen. She was not thrilled with two school-age children to rear. It was the story of Hansel and Gretel come to life. Lorraine's stepmother would give Lorraine bus money to leave, and she would leave. Then Lorraine's father would come after her, of course, and ask why she was running away. Lorraine was wise enough to know that she could not implicate her stepmother, so finally, after this game had been played out several times, Lorraine told her father that she wanted to go to live with her mother. He reluctantly allowed her and her brother, Vince, to go. Lorraine was twelve years old.

"The minute I walked in the door I knew I'd made a mistake," Lorraine sighed. "I hadn't been to my mother's for a while, and I'd forgotten what it was like. She was drunk all the time, and she and my stepfather were always fighting, and he was beating up on her, and there were all these kids getting into trouble with no one to take care of them, and it was awful."

Every Friday night when Bert, her stepfather, got paid, he'd come home with milk and steak. It would be the first time they had had anything decent to eat all week. He'd have a new dress for Lorraine's mother, and the two of them would go out dancing. They'd arrive home late, dead drunk, and the fight would be on. He'd beat up the mother, she'd call the cops, they'd haul him off to jail, and in the morning she'd go bail him out. The money would be gone, and the kids would scrounge for food for the next week until Friday, when Bert would come home with money in his pocket, milk and steak in his arms, and a new dress for Mama.

Somewhere in all of this Lorraine's mother got pregnant again, and when she went into labor, she was too drunk to realize it. Lorraine half carried, half dragged her mother down the stairs of the apartment and out to the street, where she hailed a ride from a policeman and got her mother to the hospital. Following the birth of a baby girl, the mother, Pearl, needed surgery, so Bert brought the baby home for Lorraine to name and to rear. Any hopes of high school ended right there, as Lorraine became the surrogate mother to the new baby sister.

There were now five half sisters and brothers, two battling drunken adults, and Lorraine and Vince in this household. The Friday-night wars continued, but a new twist was added: Bert began to make passes at Lorraine, who now slept in bed with a crew of kids to protect herself, with a kitchen knife under her pillow as added insurance.

On the night of a particularly savage beating, Vince threatened his mother, "If you bail him out this time, I'm leaving! This is ridiculous, and you're crazy if you let that man in here again." Vince kept his promise, and when his mother bailed Bert out in the morning, Vince left. He enlisted in the U.S. Air Force, completed school and college, and never again lived at home. He had crossed the tracks by leaps and bounds.

Meanwhile, Lorraine was guarding her life and the lives of her semi-siblings against the drunkenness and neglect of their mother and the drunkenness and violence of their father. One night Bert was not to be deterred, and as he came forcefully near Lorraine, she stabbed him. He was taken to the hospital for repair work, and she was taken by the police for protection.

"The family where I stayed was so good to me. They were gentle and they took me to church. I was so safe there. I had food, they talked nice to me, and there was this feeling of peace when I was in that beautiful church." Then the police returned to take her back home.

"As soon as I got back home I knew that my mother cared nothing for me. She was sitting on the couch. Bert was lying there with his head in her lap, and she was stroking his hair. She just looked at me with this cold look and said, 'Don't you ever hurt him again,' and I knew I was on my own."

When Lorraine was sixteen she was "purchased" by a man who had a job and a home in the South. Her mother said that he was wealthy and it would be a good idea to marry him. "He wouldn't let me have shoes. That's how he kept me. I wasn't allowed out of the house, and all I could wear were jeans and white shirts, no shoes. Eventually, as the kids were growin' a bit, he allowed me to get a job in a cotton mill. He'd come around to spy on me. If he saw me so much as speak to another man, he'd appear out of nowhere and smack me in the face, and land me clear across the other side of the room. When I'd get home, he'd take my shoes away so I couldn't leave. He kept doing this and I was scared to death. I met Eddie at the mill. I didn't know him very well—it was really his brother that I knew, but I knew that Eddie's wife had just left him for his best friend, and Eddie was upset."

Lorraine talked about her fear of her husband, how she wanted to get away, how she didn't know where to go or what to do. She wanted to take her kids somewhere for safety but knew that if she left with the kids he'd come to find her and kill her, and then the kids would have neither father nor mother. One day at work she was chatting briefly with Eddie on break when her husband appeared out of nowhere. He punched her in the head and face and threw her across the room. She was humiliated and in horrible pain. She had been saving up little bits of money that could be bus fare out of town. When she left work that day she did not go home; she walked to the local gas station to use a pay phone. She called Eddie. "I don't know why I did that—I just did. I didn't know what else to do." He told her to wait right where she was, and he would come by to get her.

When Eddie came for her, neither of them really knew what they were going to do or where they were going to go, so they headed down to the riverbank and just lived there for a while, eating fish that they could catch and "washing our hair in the river." It was the closest thing to a vacation, or even a childhood, that Lorraine had ever had. When it seemed safe to come out of hiding, Eddie informed his family that he was moving north, and he and Lorraine headed for Chicago and jobs.

I was hypnotized, but we had arrived at Tabor Church with the last carload of gifts, and it was time for worship. It was a charming morning. The children of the Tabor Sunday school put on a Christmas pageant. They had costumes made of dyed sheets, and nice props. Our people loved it. The congregation put on a lovely lunch for their people and ours. There were rows and rows of tables, people were somewhat intermingled, and there was a jolly atmosphere. Following the meal, our learning center children, under the tutelage of our teachers, Ruth and Jan, also presented a pageant. Their costumes were made up of kitchen towels, burlap, and rustic props. It was a look at the nativity from another vantage point. It was something to ponder, all right.

The people of the local congregation left at this point. Reverend Jim as the Santa, with help from his two elves, Reverend Mick and Reverend Tom, passed out the presents. It was fun and funny, and there was an abundance of "stuff," with something for everybody and multiple gifts for all the children. But there were problems. The woman who sat across from me at the table was angry and envious about the gifts that some of the children got because her daughter got "three teddy bears, and she doesn't need three teddy bears! Why didn't she get a doll? or some boots? or a jacket?"

It was hard not to be annoyed, not to say standard things such as, "You should be grateful. . . ." Yet it really was a frustration to try to figure out how to make things come out even. People gave gifts in good faith. How could we be better stewards of these gifts?

The whole party ended around two, and I was eager to get people back and things transported, because as Sunday school teacher and youth group counselor at my own church, I had to be there for our pageant at four o'clock.

With Lorraine in the middle and Martha, the navigator, at the window seat, and the kids in back, we headed back to The Ministry building carrying their gifts, and I asked Martha how she had happened to come to The Ministry. It was around Christmastime two years before. Richard, her husband, had been working as a roofer. Then he came down with appendicitis, was hospitalized, and had surgery. That meant he was out of work. Meanwhile, Martha had been hospitalized with sarcoidosis, a severe lung disease, and had nearly died. They had four young children at this point: Crystal, who was six; Donna, five; Sharon, three; and Richie, one. There was no work and no money, and they needed food.

"I had heard about The Ministry, and I walked around the block three times before I got the nerve to go in. Finally, I went in and met Reverend Tom. He gave me a bag of food but also took my name and address and the ages of the kids. It was just before Christmas, and of course we didn't have anything. One day there was a knock at the door, and when I went to open it, there were these people from the suburbs. They had a tree with all the decorations, stuff for Christmas dinner with all the trimmings, and presents for each of the kids, including some new clothes, plus stuff for me and Richard. I'd never seen anything like it. It was the best Christmas we ever had, and after that I came back to help out. Richard got to working again, and things were sort of okay and I wanted to do something to help. There are so many people around here who need so much help—who are a lot worse off than we were—I just felt I needed to do something somehow. And here was a place, finally, where people didn't just talk about religion, but lived out their faith in Jesus. That's when I came back to the church. You know, Lynn, it's amazing how God really takes care of people. I wish I knew more about that. You know, I'd like to learn something about prayer."

We arrived at the building and unloaded Lorraine and her children and their gifts, and then I drove Martha the two remaining blocks to her home, bade her farewell, and headed north to my own church. I was churning with oral history, heady with energy from all the comings and goings, hyped up for yet another celebration, but pondering. Martha wanted to know something about prayer. She was hungry for a new journey—a journey in faith. How could I help?

I hopped from the car and greeted my husband, who was glad that I'd arrived in time. In the youth group room, the boys and girls were getting dressed and made up for the pageant. Our own children were adjusting their costumes—Andrew an angel in white, Bonnie a shepherd in blue, and Amy in a children's choir collar. Lookin' good! My Sunday school class was lined up, a multi-colored clan of shepherds, and I went upstairs to take a seat in the congregation. I was sitting down, I was off duty, and I eased back in the pew to absorb the aesthetics of the afternoon. It was going on four o'clock and getting dark. The candlelight in the church gave a subdued patina to the rough stone walls. The tiny white lights on the two tall chancel Christmas trees winked against the tinsel, and the chords of the organ helped me relax and soothe the sore place in the small of my back.

The pageant began, and for the third time that day the story unfolded, but this time the tiny angels were very washed, very white, with perfectly symmetrical golden halos. This choir had matching white blouses and shirts under the large red collars; the herald angel had enormous wings that emanated from somewhere behind the elegant robe; Mary and Joseph were more regal than impoverished; and the kings were dressed in long velvet garments with coordinated crowns. It was magnificent. It was nourishing to my senses. It was polished. I was exhausted. Somehow this all fit together, but I'd think about it later. There was a potluck supper followed by caroling at the nursing homes. My husband, Scott, and I could talk tonight after the children were in bed. Meanwhile, this niggling question from Martha: Was there something that I could teach her about prayer?

Oreste

$\mathcal{S}$ki-slope nose, legs crossed casually, sly grin on his face, he sang out at the top of his lungs, "Roll on, big mama," and laughed and laughed and laughed, and sang the refrain again. People near him got angry and hollered at him to keep still. Oreste was a lonely old man who got attention by aggravating people. He would come to The Ministry and sit around in the afternoon, and when it was terribly noisy or dead quiet, would suddenly bellow forth with the one phrase of the song—then laugh, mutter, and say, "Baaaah" after someone would holler, "Shut up, old man."

One day as he sat slurping his coffee, he began to bawl. "Peewee died. My cat. Ah—she used to open and close the light." He sat and yowled. My daughter Bonnie wanted to take him a kitten, so we visited him and he eagerly embraced Peewee the Second. His apartment, in a relatively decent building, was a hovel. It was in the cellar beyond the boiler room, and the whole area stank. When I tried to open the window to alleviate the stench and the stifling heat, I discovered that it was nailed shut. The landlord's rage and challenge when I approached him about it frightened me: "What has that old man been telling you?" he fumed.

Later, on one of Martha's days at work, I slid into a chair by her desk and said that we needed to talk about Oreste. I described the oven that was his apartment, the maniacal landlord, the putrid smell, and the not-so-cheery knowledge that the landlord now recognized me and spotted me for a problem after my comment about opening Oreste's window.

We discussed other buildings in the area—which ones were for families only, which were too expensive, which had vacancies, and which were strictly walk-ups. There were not many options. Oreste was in his seventies, had a minor heart condition, was relatively quiet, but had very poor personal hygiene. Martha said she'd check some things out but that possibly her own landlady would allow Oreste to have the small apartment in the basement of her building.

This would all have to be done very prudently, as once the landlord of Oreste's current apartment discovered he was leaving, he could make things difficult for Oreste. Oreste's landlord had a good thing going. The building was pretty much a singles-only building, with maybe two or three apartments for two, and it housed about fifty people. The manager would take a person's entire general assistance, SSI (Supplemental Security Income), or Social Security check, plus all food stamps, and in return keep a soup kettle going. For the resident who always drank up a check or traded food stamps for cash for booze—the Uptown version of the triangle trade route—this was a good practice. No one would die of starvation. It wasn't just, however, because the amount of food didn't nearly equal what was due a person, and the process of securing the food stamps was akin to extortion.

In a few days Martha brought good news: The apartment was vacant and the landlady would agree to have Oreste. There was one glitch—bugs. Martha and I guessed that Oreste might have lice. He would have to be removed from his current residence at the beginning of the month (just before his Social Security check came), then bathed and not returned to the site of probable infestation before being moved to his new address. Chances were that very little from his old place would accompany him.

Martha had energy like no one else I knew and would tackle tasks that no one else would; she also had an amazing capacity to tolerate the gross. Martha could even deal with Oreste. She purchased soap and shampoo for delousing and took him home to give him a bath. He screamed bloody murder, throwing a fit at the notion of being stripped down, but Martha prevailed. The compromise was that she allowed him to keep his underwear on, then put his creaky old bones in her modified cauldron of a bathtub. Her description of the struggle was worthy of any stand-up comic, but the description of Oreste's body belonged in a pathology report. He was covered with sores and scratches and bites and welts. His body was a real road map of marks. Before winter, Oreste was securely moved into his newly painted, tiny apartment. He was safe, close to Martha, who could keep a trained eye on him, and even a half block closer to our office. It was great for several months.

The scene repeated itself in reverse when Martha found me on my day at work (we were both part-time staff people, working most days in common) and slid into a chair next to my desk. "Lynn, my landlady's having a fit. We've got to get Oreste out of the apartment. It's a filthy mess, it smells, Oreste is a mess, there's rotting food everywhere, garbage all over the place—and he can't stay. The man needs a keeper. What're we gonna do now?"

"Okay, Marth, give me a little time." Think, think, think. Pace, pace, pace. "I'll come up with something, and in the meantime, tell your landlady we'll get him out."

It was a food day, so that occupied the whole morning. Bringing the charts up to date carried over into the afternoon a bit, but after a late lunch of yogurt, I hit the street and walked north to the Somerset House. In its youth it had been a pleasant building, with the Edgewater Beach Hotel and the famous Aragon Ballroom as neighborhood companions, but no more. The Edgewater Beach had been torn down. The Aragon remained, but no Big Band sound with tuxedoed clientele ventured into this semi-safe neighborhood, parts of which were safe by day but deadly at night.

The Somerset was now a community care home, a level-three home, a sheltered home—different names apply, depending on state regulations, but it means it was safe, meals were served, different levels of care were offered on different floors, and a prescribed level of nursing care, social service intervention, and activities were available. Oreste would have a room instead of an apartment, but there would be laundry done for him, meals provided, and his health could be monitored in a minor way, as allowed for by the state regulations that licensed institutions of this type.

I met with the social worker, gave her my card, explained a bit about The Ministry, how I knew Oreste, what his background and current needs were. She was understanding, willing to take him, and had an opening, but he would need a medical workover to comply with the state regulations.

Martha made the medical arrangements and pacified her landlady with promises to clean the apartment as soon as Oreste vacated it, and once again Oreste moved. He was hospitalized for four days for observation and a medical work-up. After that he was given a green light for the level of care provided at the Somerset, and things were stable again.

The snow and ice were gone now, and it was easy to get out and walk, which Oreste enjoyed. Once adjusted to his new surroundings, he walked the several blocks south to our office to stop in for coffee in the afternoon and sit and have a smoke. He smoked Pall Malls when he had the money, clippers when he didn't. Lots of people smoked clippers—butts collected from the streets, ashtrays, anywhere. Some people even carried a coffee can to collect the butts. They'd remove the old paper by rolling the butt between a thumb and middle finger to extract the tobacco, then pour the tobacco into a can and use cigarette papers to create new "rolls," as they were called. People who were good at this could crease the paper, pour in the tobacco, roll it up, lick the side, press it shut, and put it to the lips in one slick operation with one hand. Aficionados of this practice showed me the best way to do it: first, roll a paper around a pencil; then reopen the paper, shake in the tobacco, tamp it down, lick the paper, and reroll it. The pencil was a fancy trick.

Oreste was not an aficionado. He just pleated the paper, made a cigarette, and smoked it down to nothing. If we were lucky, he didn't drop the butt on the floor and grind it into the carpet with his shoe to extinguish it.

Oreste loved dairy products. Many years earlier he had been told that he had an ulcer and should drink cream. He would buy cartons of half-and-half coffee cream and chug them down, and he loved milk, pudding, and ice cream—more, perhaps, because he had no teeth.

He hung around a lot now that he was in his new spot, and he was cleaner, but he was annoyed with his living situation. He'd come into the building and yell, "Lee, Lee, where's-a Lee?" That was me.

On these nice days of early summer I'd walk him back to his building when I was ready to leave the office. I'd take the A train instead of the B—it was a bit out of my way, and connections were not quite as good, but it was the stop near Oreste's place. There was also a drugstore on the corner, and I'd buy two ice cream bars or two ice cream sandwiches or prefrozen cones, and we'd saunter up Sheridan Road, licking the ice cream. It was a pleasant way to end the day.

Oreste would introduce me to people who stopped to chat with him, "This is my daughter, Lee, a-hmm," or on occasion he would even introduce me as his wife! Sometimes people's eyebrows would shoot up and take me in with a question mark. I'd close my eyes and make the slightest gesture to demur, and the startled expression would be squelched. At other times I didn't bother to correct Oreste. It just didn't matter very much. He was happy about it. Sometimes it didn't seem odd to the person inquiring, and it didn't hurt me any. It was our little game—it was amusing. At the Somerset, my name and office and home phone numbers were the numbers listed to call in an emergency anyway, so as the years passed it seemed less odd.

On one particularly bright, sunny July afternoon Oreste and I headed north licking ice cream bars. It was one of the rare times that Oreste didn't seem like my sheep, like a lost person who was strange, like a character. He talked about the Somerset, and how he hated to go back there. He hated the food, and they wouldn't give him "extra milk"! It was the only thing he asked for—over and over and over—two milks with his meals, and pudding. A frequent question on his agenda was whether my husband beat me. "Ah, duz-a-yur hoosban' beat you?" No, Oreste, I'd tell him. "M-m, aha!" "Oreste, did you beat your wife?" I'd ask him. "M-m, only little bit." We had this same conversation, over and over and over.

It began like that on this day, but I heard something else. I was watching the cracks of the sidewalk and recognized myself playing the childhood game: "If you step on a crack, you'll break your mother's back. If you step on a line, you'll break your mother's spine." What was I doing? I was carefully stepping over the odd mess of sidewalk, then doing all lines and cracks, then counting how many steps in a square. It didn't match my stride, but if I took three steps so that my last step was close to the line, then two steps in the next square with the last step about two-thirds the distance into the square, then the first step of the next square would be close to the beginning, and it would work—three, two, three, two, whoops—missed one, back in step here. Something about this concentration on my steps sharpened my ears to what Oreste was saying.

"Nobody loves me, nobody wants to kiss me, so I act like a crazy old man singing songs in Italian."

What? Say what? Was Oreste telling me that this was all an act? How much did he really know about his behavior? How helpless was he, really? And who on earth was I? I was thirty-seven years old, a mother of three who lived in the suburbs, had led a rather sheltered life, was not a professional person, had lucked into a job I loved, and here I was walking this old man back to a place that I'd got him into, a place he hated, did not want to be. I'd made the arrangements, and he was stuck. I was no kin to him. What right did I have to do this? Nobody loved him—but he wanted someone to love him; nobody wanted to kiss him—but he wanted somebody to kiss him; so he acted crazy, and I'd scooped him up off the street, clipped his wings, assumed responsibility for where he'd live, and bought him off with an ice cream. If I could do this to Oreste, could somebody do this to me someday?

Floyd

Rarely did I drive to work—it was a pain. I took the el and read, which was my R & R, but it was August 20, Arthur's birthday. On this day I drove because I'd brought Arthur's birthday cake—raspberry, so it would be pink, Arthur's favorite color. Arthur was in his late twenties, a slightly built man we had thought to be retarded. Abandoned by his mother when he was eight, Arthur was a very angry man, with much buried grief, a beautiful tenor singing voice, and inordinate tenderness toward children. Arthur was worth the aggravation of driving into the city. It was a food day, which meant a busy and hectic morning and an afternoon celebration of Arthur's birthday. It would be a no-break-for-lunch day, but a fun day, a fast-moving day.

Floyd's chart was next in the stack, and I picked it up, checked when he'd been in for food last, and walked down the stairs to call his name. An easy food interview. That was the thing about Floyd. Whoever interviewed him would feel good because Floyd would be gracious, and he made the staff person feel useful and worthwhile. Floyd was easy. Actually, he was an enigma. A man of few words, things were always "fine" and he was always "grateful," but he was guarded. Floyd would have blended into any standard WASP community, one of the things that made him stand out in Uptown Chicago.

"Good morning, Floyd. How are you today?"

"Well . . ." Silence.

That's odd. "You're very quiet today."

"Yes." He sat there—neat and presentable, very Scandinavian-looking and dignified, but he didn't say a word. It seemed as though he was struggling with language, but nothing came out.

"Do you need to talk about something, Floyd?"

"I don't want to bother you."

"Floyd, that's what I'm here for. To listen to you. There's nothing else that I'm supposed to be doing right now except be with you."

I waited and waited. Seconds. A minute. Two minutes. It seemed like hours, but then he said, "It's too much to talk about."

I sat back in the chair and tried to appear relaxed, as if I had until the weekend. The crowd downstairs, others waiting for food, might be making him feel reluctant to take my time. Another minute went by. Floyd bent his head.

"My dog died last night."

"Oh, Floyd, I'm sorry to hear that."

He looked up at me now. "I don't know what to do."

"Yes," I said. "I can imagine. That's very sad."

"What I mean is, I don't know what to do! She was seventeen years old. A little chihuahua. She was such a good dog—like a child to me. But what will I do with her? Last week a dog got hit in the street, and they just threw it in the garbage truck when it drove by. I don't want to do that with my dog. She's like a child! I don't want to bury her in a vacant lot—kids might dig her up—or other dogs. I just don't know what to do. . . ." His voice faded, and he sat there quietly with tears in his eyes. His dog had died.

"Just a minute, Floyd—excuse me." I slipped into Smitty's office. I had a weird idea, and I wondered if it were even legal. Oh, Smitty, be in a good mood, dear friend.

"Smitty, I have a wild favor to ask. Smitty, can we bury a dog in the backyard?" His eyebrows went up and his jaw went down, but he didn't yell. I slipped into a chair and rapidly whispered about Floyd. Smitty was a softy. In brave moments I dared to call him "Marshmallow." He also loved my dog, so the subject matter was good. He just stared for a minute, then said, "Tell Richard to dig a hole," shook his head, and went back to his paper work.

I hurried back into the next room where Floyd sat. "Floyd, Smitty says that we can bury your dog here at The Ministry. How's that?"

Floyd sat up with relief. Words were lost in the details, but the arrangement was that I would pick him up, with his dog, at one P.M., and he could bury the dog. I wrote out a food slip, handed it to him, told him I'd see him at one, and ran down the back stairs to talk with Richard Grooms, Martha's husband. Richard was busy bagging up groceries for the people who had come for the food. I took him aside, briefly recounting Floyd's story, and asked if he'd dig the hole. Richard was accommodating. With his mellow, warm manner and a Georgia accent, Richard had come to work with us shortly after our move to the new building. He really enjoyed the unusual requests, and this was surely a first.

We finished the food process, and the staff all gathered downstairs around twelve thirty to sing happy birthday to Arthur and have some cake. Arthur was pleased, and some people had some gifts for him—another coffee mug, a new pipe, some tobacco, cards. Somebody made the mistake of asking his age, and he had a minor tantrum. "You know I never discuss my age!" But that all got smoothed over with some more cake. Then it was time to get Floyd.

How convenient that my car was here today! The thought of walking five city blocks carrying a dead dog almost made me swoon. I hadn't told Floyd that I was phobic about dead things.

I had never visited Floyd before. His building looked quite nice for the neighborhood. It was a courtyard building, and Floyd's apartment was down the path, the last entrance on the left. Inside the vestibule I searched vainly for a name long ago obliterated on the mailboxes. I was about to guess at the buzzers when Floyd appeared. He'd been watching and had seen me from his window. We walked up the half flight of stairs to his first-floor apartment, where his wife met us at the door. We were introduced. Then he ushered me in and over to the corner of the living room, where he had a small dresser drawer sitting on a chair. He said, "Here's my dog." The small brown dog was neatly resting on some cloth inside the drawer, carefully covered with a woman's rose-colored sweater, meticulously tucked around the dog's neck. It was the way a child would fix a doll.

I caught my breath to keep from fainting dead away. "That's very nice, Floyd." Don't swoon, Lynn—just get out of here. As I turned and made busy mutterings about leaving, I could see Floyd out of the corner of my eye busying himself putting a final covering over the dresser drawer. I held the door open and walked in front of him so as not to see the box. This is ridiculous, Lynn—it's just a phobia; control yourself, breathe.

We drove back to The Ministry, Floyd sitting next to me in the front seat with the BOX. Don't think about the BOX. Don't think about what's in the BOX. Concentrate on the road. I pulled over into a space in front of The Ministry, and we got out and walked around to the back of the building.

Richard was there by a freshly dug hole, shovel against a tree, and four chairs in front of the hole. It seemed so melodramatic and heavy and comical all at the same time that I kept swallowing and blinking imaginary tears or laughter, and I didn't even know which. I did know that I didn't want to see the dog again, even as Floyd was repeating the ceremony of showing his pet to Richard. Richard was patient and didn't swoon, and when Floyd was finished, he tacked a lid on the drawer. On top of the lid was a crucifix. He carefully placed the box in Richard's small grave. Then Richard picked up the shovel, dumped in a load of dirt, and handed the shovel to me. This was a "high ceremony" funeral! I handed the shovel to Floyd, and we went round until the hole was filled. Afterward, Floyd was content to sit in the yard in one of the chairs. It was really a graceful yard for this area—probably the only yard like it in blocks. It was grassy, with bushes by the fence and a few old trees. The shade was comforting in the August heat of a Chicago summer, and there was a gentle breeze. I went inside.

Eventually Floyd came in. "Would you like some birthday cake, Floyd?" He accepted readily, and also the offer of a cup of tea.

Floyd, born in Davenport, Iowa, was living with his wife Virginia. They had no children. On this day, with the tenderness of a nurturing parent, he buried his seventeen-year-old dog.

Violet

*V*iolet had a face I'd seen before: the face of Rosie the Riveter as she appears in documentaries. Violet's was a face in the factory, a face in the crowd, and definitely a 1940s face in black and white. The hairdo was 1943 Ann Sheridan—bangs, curls, below the ears but above the shoulders—and she had lines and crinkles. She smiled easily, but pain leaked out the sides of her eyes, and she walked with weariness as her companion. She had probably been very pretty at nineteen, and with a different husband in a different era she would have been next-door neighbor U.S.A.

This was the 1970s, though, and Violet had not escaped a hard life. She was a devout Roman Catholic, her face was familiar in the community, and she seemed immune to harm. If people spoke of her, it was in the tones reserved for those to whom sainthood was ascribed. She stood in line to eat breakfast at the Salvation Army, she stood in line to get groceries from us at The Ministry, and she stood in line for the Wednesday night spaghetti suppers at St. Thomas of Canterbury Roman Catholic Church. Violet was long on patience.

Violet was married to Bill, her husband of twenty-some years. He was a veteran of World War II and one of the people who led me to understand what Jesus meant when he said, "The poor you always have with you." As long as the possibility of disease, accidents, wars, or violence existed, people would get broken and bear the scars. Bill bore the scars of the brain-damaged alcoholic and thus was a double victim: a victim of disease and a victim of war.

One time when they were in for food and I was interviewing them, Bill was talking along and suddenly in midsentence was off on an entirely different sentence with a different topic and time. I thought maybe I'd dozed off or missed something and asked him to repeat himself. As I drew him out a bit and looked at the details on the chart, I noticed that he was a veteran and directed the conversation to that. Yes, he was a veteran, all right; yes, he'd been a tail gunner, uh-huh; and he'd been shot in the head, m-m, and had a metal plate right back here—turning his head about thirty degrees to the left and inclining his forehead a bit as he pointed to the spot where the plate was.

I looked at him a bit differently after that. I could sit in that chair, a free woman, because that man was walking around with metal in his head. Who was the servant, really? What a crock it was to think that I was there taking care of him by giving him a scant bag of groceries that had been donated by someone else. This man gave the best part of his life! He gave his youth and his right mind; his sons and his wife were left with a lot less of a man than Bill might have been.

Bill, like many other veterans, did not return from the war whole, but neither was he neatly dead so that we could play taps once a year, place a wreath, and eat ice cream after watching the parade on our day off. He wasn't even damaged enough to be conveniently warehoused in a VA hospital where our groups could visit, distribute candy and cigarettes, and go away for a year. Bill was among us, talking nonsense, staggering drunk, and needing food. He had red hair, flaky white skin with a florid cast, and a puffing kind of talk.

Violet and Bill had two boys. The elder was very limited mentally and the younger was an incorrigible, a constant truant from school. At thirteen he had become a runaway, and Violet would request food for only three, since only one son was home. She was upset, of course, but also wearily resigned to his absence. The boy had been a handful, and she had not known what to do with him. Over a period of two years she spoke of someone's having seen him in the park or of a friend's telling her that she'd seen him in a diner or passed him on the street. Violet herself reported two or three sightings of her own, where she had seen him at a distance. He'd looked at her and run like a frightened deer. It was like UFO talk—all unconfirmed.

Many nights during the era of Mayor Richard J. Daley, both the five o'clock Chicago news and the six o'clock network news broadcasts carried many of the same stories. The night the lead story was about serial killer John Wayne Gacy was one of those nights. Gacy, a local suburban pretender to public office, photographed on the fringes of this or that political gathering, was shown handcuffed, being led out of his suburban brick bungalow. The details of the story were gross.

Following a missing-persons report, a team had gone into Gacy's home with a search warrant and begun to uncover bodies buried in a crawl space under the house. The entire city and suburban populations were gripped by the grotesque and macabre details and were riveted to the news in fascinated horror. As the story unfolded over a period of days and weeks, the final count of bodies recovered totaled twenty-nine from the house and four that had been thrown in the river.

The bodies were all young males between the ages of eleven and eighteen, a majority in their early adolescence. They were all of slight build and had been sexually molested. John Gacy was a large man, married and divorced many years earlier. He admitted to being a homosexual and a pedophile at the time of his arrest. He had been well liked, was often in the company of children, and had a reputation for giving large parties for children at local organizations and community centers. He was considered to be a clown—funny, jolly, generous, and popular.

That following week Violet was in for food, and this time she was interviewed by Martha. A very sober-faced Martha came out of her office. "I've sent Violet to the Boys Clubs of America building up on Sheridan Road. They provide dental care in this neighborhood for poor children, and I told Violet to go get her son's dental records and take them down to the morgue. I just have this feeling that her son is one of those boys."

Within the week Violet returned. Her son was the eleventh body recovered from the crawl space.

John

*D*ear John. He had a way of absenting himself from holiday festivities and other special events. His absence would be noted, but the occasions were too hectic to track him down and issue the special invitation his low self-esteem and shyness required. Everyone liked John and would have been glad to find him. Time was the barrier.

So it happened that again John missed all the Christmas festivities at The Ministry. It was a shame, for things had been especially nice this year. It was our first year at the new building, a wonderful old house with stained-glass windows, a turret on the third floor, and a backyard with a garage. The garage became the food storage pantry. The back porch held a freezer; the basement was painted with outrageously jolly colors and was the learning center and pre-school place; the kitchen on the first floor always had a large coffee-pot going; and the living and dining room areas were used for worship, Bible class, mother's group, learning center after-school activities, Saturday dinners, general drop-in-for-a-cup-of-coffee area, and the waiting area on food distribution mornings.

We had a piano, the windows were large and let in a lot of light, there was nice old woodwork, and even fireplaces, so the atmosphere was very homey. The second-floor bedrooms were used for offices, and the third-floor apartment was living space for a staff person, Milt Smith.

The Christmas festivities were organized differently this year. We held four open houses, at six thirty in the evening, during the week before Christmas. We sang, had cookies, cakes, punch, coffee, and crackers and cheese, and distributed gifts to everyone. All these things were donated by our supporters, and for weeks we received packages of homemade cookies, bars, squares, and cakes in the mail from Wisconsin, Iowa, Michigan, and Indiana. It was astonishing. People from local area congregations drove in with things and would visit, but the mail was always dazzling. We would get the occasional coffee can filled with bourbon balls so heavily saturated that the kitchen smelled like a barroom. Of course, the staff was forced to consume them on the spot. Later newsletters warned donors that rum balls and bourbon balls would not be a good idea for a heavily alcoholic clientele, but their arrival did give us a good laugh when it happened.

Sign-up sheets were used for these open houses. A person could come only one time, and after the first year we set a limit of fifty people per evening. It was really a warm and wonderful time— fun and festive, the type of social gathering that no one in this impoverished community had access to except through us. The staff took turns hosting these events in twos and threes, and we mixed men and women. It could be necessary to bounce someone who was drunk and obnoxious—it happened once or twice—and an extra person in charge was a must.

It was this warmth and hospitality that John missed. He dropped in one day in mid-January after the decorations were gone except for a stray angel forgotten on a mantel and a bit of tinsel that the carpet sweeper had missed. It was shortly before closing time. He was waiting to see me; he didn't want anything—had just come to say hello. He was given a cup of coffee, and when I was free I went into the living room to visit with him. He was wearing his big black shoes and gray socks, gray pants, and a hooded navy blue zippered sweatshirt.

"Good afternoon, Mrs. Perry," he said, rising to his feet, clicking his heels together, bowing, saluting, and extending his long arm to shake hands in one continuous action. This was usually accompanied by a German military phrase of some kind and an embarrassed, furtive smile. I sat and visited with him a bit. He knew it was the end of office hours and agreed to walk out with me on my way to the train. Since he lived a few blocks south, I said I'd walk his way and take the train at Wilson Avenue rather than the Lawrence Avenue train, which would mean walking north.

I ran upstairs to grab my coat and purse, and then detoured by the closet to see if any Christmas packages were left. Most of the leftovers we had given to area nursing homes or taken to Save the Alcoholic or given in food parcels or home visits. I found one small item wrapped in green tissue paper and took it downstairs with me.

I said good night to the troops and walked out with John. As I pulled the door closed behind me I said, "John, here's something for you from The Ministry. Everyone missed you at Christmastime—you missed all the parties—but here's a little present for you anyway."

We continued to walk to the corner and around to the left when we came to Sheridan. We talked and walked, John matching stride as he opened his small parcel. He tore away the paper, which floated to the sidewalk, and held up a key ring, hissing at me. His lip curled a bit, and he sneered. "What am I supposed to do with this, Mrs. Perry? Here's my key!" His left hand went to his chest, where he fished a key out from inside his shirt. He had one key, the key to his apartment, hanging on a string tied around his neck. He let the key flap free and tossed the key ring into a vacant lot on his left.

The movement cut a slice inside me and prompted a gasp, which I suppressed. My first thought was waste. Instantly that changed to: Poor John, now he has nothing. What a paradox—a person in need and a person needing to give, but instead of meeting, the needs had breezed by like lanes of north and south traffic at rush hour. I felt pity at the wasted gift—had a child picked it out and bought it with allowance money? Had a retired person purchased it from small Social Security funds? Where had it come from?

Dear John. Forgotten. He forgot about Christmas. A forgetter forgotten. Now reminded, hope of a gift rekindled the possibility of having been remembered; but no luck, he had missed out again. Hope smashed may be worse than no hope at all. It teases. Poor John. Dear John. What to do? How to wed the generous with the needy—the giver with the recipient?

The dilemma was a splinter in my mind. I picked and picked at it and squeezed it. It got sore, subsided, returned, and somewhere nicked a memory—the memory of grade school and preparing Christmas gifts for veterans. What did we do? The teacher in each class provided a shoebox. Children were encouraged to bring things to fill the shoeboxes, which would then be delivered to the Veterans Home.

Shoeboxes! Why not? People could fill shoeboxes with consumable items—an orange, pocket Kleenex, raisin boxes, hard candy, Chap Stick, gum, a pair of socks, mittens, Life Savers, a deck of cards, disposable razors, soap, toothbrush, a pocket comb, and so forth.

The idea took. Each year a staff person refined the idea—designate a package for a man or a woman, wrap the packages, wrap the top and bottom separately so we could peek in and perhaps mix things up if we needed more women's packages or more men's packages; if you wanted to give something extra special, such as a pocket radio, mark the box accordingly.

This project became a huge success. Supporters really liked the idea. Everyone could participate in it, and it was relatively foolproof. It made life simpler for the staff. Shoeboxes could be stacked, so storage and distribution were smooth, and it provided the most equitable gifts. As the years went by, there were shoeboxes for all the open houses, home visits, food people, and nursing home folks—well over five hundred boxes each Christmas.

Whenever I hear the word "shoebox," I think of the inspiration for this project: John and his sardonic dismissal of the key ring. When I think of the dollar key chain thrown in the vacant lot, I like to think of it not as wasted, but as a seed—the seed that finally let us find a way to match the needs of the giver and the needs of the recipient.

Julie

           I loved Chicago in January when it got very cold. Those subzero, bright-blue-sky days were beautiful. The snow was over everything, the frozen shoreline of Lake Michigan creating huge new landscapes of water, sand, ice, and snow. The air was invigorating, the brilliance was exhilarating, and the walks to the train and bus were welcome forays into winter—as long as there was no wind.

It was just such a morning as this that Julie arrived for food with Terence and Emily in tow, neither child wearing mittens. Julie popped up the stairs while I was pulling the files and, smiling at me, passed in front of me to put something wrapped in a paper napkin on my desk.

"This is for you, young lady," she grinned, and went back down the stairs.

I drew in my breath, sighed, and looked over. There on the desk was half a grapefruit—part of Julie's Salvation Army breakfast. Julie lived at 5220 North these days, and the Salvation Army was 4600 North—six city blocks. We were 4800 North, and another two blocks east. It was twenty degrees below zero, and her kids weren't wearing mittens despite the fact that she'd probably been given many pairs. She walked to the Salvation Army for breakfast at six in the morning, and she was now here for food before half past eight. If she could get things together enough to do all that, why, oh, why couldn't she use her food stamps for food? How could I make her understand?

Frustration. The name of my torment was frustration. I was almost never depressed—but frustrated? Often. I would ask over and over and over, "If Julie is so clever, how can she be so stupid? Is she retarded? What is it? Can she be taught?" I was reduced to helplessness.

Alcoholism was a big problem in Uptown. Julie herself did not drink, but the rotating trio of men with whom she lived did. If she gave the food stamps to the men and they sold them, did we dare deny food when it was the children who would suffer?

When I spoke with Julie about her need to come for groceries for the third time this month, I insisted that something had to change. We discussed what she did when her check came and how the very first thing she was supposed to do with those food stamps was to buy food! I told her that she would receive food today, and we wanted to be certain that the children were fed. We would shop with her, or for her if necessary, but she was going to buy those children food. Since her check came on the third of the month, I told her that Martha and I would come to her apartment on the fourth of the following month to see how she was managing. We would expect to see food! She gave her usual, "Yes, young lady," answer, yet all the while I dreaded what would happen.

I wrote on my desk calendar "See Julie" in the square for the fourth of the following month, guiltily pitched the grapefruit, and told Martha about the interview and our "appointment." I talked over Julie's situation with Reverend Jim, and discussed it in staff meetings. I prayed about it and obsessed about it. What a mess!

Two weeks later, on a gray winter afternoon, Martha and I headed north to Julie's apartment. She did not answer our knock, and we checked with the building manager to be sure we had the right apartment. "Oh, most of the time she's hangin' out with that guy Carlo downstairs in 320."

I gave Martha the eye, and she glared back at me. Couldn't be. Someone opened the door of 320 at our knock, and the entrance was right at the foot of a double bed, occupied by Julie and Carlo. They were dressed, just lying there watching television, but when Julie saw us she scowled. We reminded her that we had come to see the food she had bought, as agreed upon.

Julie got up from the bed, with Terence and Emily following her, and stormed out of the apartment toward the elevator. When we reached her apartment, she pulled the key from inside her shirt and opened the door. It was not the worst apartment I had ever seen because it was almost empty, but what was there was awful. There was a front room, a bedroom, a kitchen, and a bathroom.

The front room was empty except for a pile of clothing in the corner and a bare single mattress on the floor. There was also a stroller.

The bedroom had a double bed with a filthy white sheet. Not only yellowed and just plain dirty, it was stained with blood and urine. There were no blankets.

The bathtub was black. It looked like a tub where a muddy dog had been bathed. There was standing water in the bathroom sink.

The kitchen was amazing. I had often used the phrase, "There's nothing in my refrigerator." When children say, "The refrigerator is empty—there's nothing to eat," it usually means, There's nothing good in here, or There's nothing that I want. Julie's refrigerator was empty. Absolutely nothing was in there—not even ice. No ketchup. No mustard. No leftovers. Nothing with mold on it. Not an apple, or a pickle, or a bottle of milk. Empty. There was a jar of mayonnaise and a bottle of prune juice on the counter. In the cabinet was a box of Cream of Wheat and a package of Hamburger Helper. The cupboard was bare.

We were stunned, but finally did tell a very sullen Julie that we hoped she would do better next month and we would be back then. The worst shock had been to see Carlo with Julie and the children. He was well known to the staff. A mean and disgusting man, he was a heavy drinker. The street gossip about him was that once, when drunk, he had urinated in a baby bottle and made his kids drink it. This was not a man to be in the company of Terence and Emily.

I had once asked the caseworker why they had not taken Terence and Emily when Jill, the baby, had been taken. The other two were obviously at risk as well. "You are my eyes and ears," I'd been told. "You put me on the scene—describe what you see so I can see it too. Put me on the spot, and that means document, document, document."

Back in the office, I pulled Julie's file. I went into my office, closed the door, and pulled out some paper. This report needed to be very detailed and very accurate.

As impossible as it seemed to be to instill in Julie her need to use her food stamps for food, she perhaps now understood that we would persist in checking because Julie was noticeably absent from our office. None of the staff had seen her, no one we asked had seen her on the street, and inquiries of our counterparts at other local pantries drew blanks also.

Many weeks later, while pulling files for the morning's food interviews, I was aware of extra noise and confusion downstairs. It was Julie, with Terence and Emily. The place was packed, and she was noisily greeting folks and helping to serve coffee. Helpfulness was Julie's way of coercing others to bend the rules. It was toward the end of the month, and Julie wanted food. Even though we had a capacity list, her name was added to it.

When it was her turn to be interviewed, I walked down the stairs to greet her and accompany her to my office.

"And how are you, young lady?" she beamed at me toothlessly, while placing a paper-napkin-wrapped danish on my desk in one long swooping motion.

I was instantly tired. All the frustration associated with Julie flooded into my consciousness. The list of questions with no answers engulfed me as I looked at her smiling face.

"Good morning, Julie. Haven't seen you for a long time. I spoke with Sister Rose a few weeks ago, and she said you're back with Emily's dad, Jeff. Is that right?"

Julie smiled with lips pressed together, then shut her eyes and shook her head slowly from side to side, looking very smug.

"Nope. Wallace. I'm staying with Wallace now."

"You're back with Wallace?"

"Yup. Me an' him are gonna stay together this time."

Wallace, much older than Julie, had grown children somewhere. When sober, he was an immaculate housekeeper. Drunk, he was mean, quarrelsome, and physically abusive to Terence. She was now living only two blocks away, though, and with luck it would be easier to oversee things and be of help. I buzzed the learning center and talked with Jan. Terence and Emily were old enough for preschool now, and, miraculously, there was an opening and Jan would accept them. A new avenue to help the children! Julie liked the idea too, and she would go to talk with Jan in the learning center after leaving my office.

Again we returned to the discussion of her food stamps. Oh, yes, young lady, she knew all about that, and of course she would buy food. Again I advised her that Martha and I would come by to help her remember. Hm-m, hum-m, yes, she would of course buy food. I tore off a food slip from the pad, filled in the information, and handed it to Julie. I reminded her to talk with Jan about preschool and said good-bye. After she left, I just sat there for a minute trying to summon the energy to get up, even to close her file folder. I sat up straight, turned the sheets to the face sheets, changed the address, wrote Wallace's name at the top under Julie's, and placed the folder on top of the stack of those I'd seen so far this morning, waiting to do the charting until after all the food people had been served.

Julie was now back in the swing of things, apparently feeling herself to be "in favor" with us once again, and she dropped in on the way back and forth to here and there. Julie was always "on the way." Either she was scurrying with an armload of baby clothes that she got somewhere to take to someone who had a new baby, or she was on her way with the children to the Salvation Army for breakfast. Two nights a week the Salvation Army served supper, and a third night she ate at St. Thomas's. She would attend worship on occasion, often with the children. I could not get my brains around the person of Julie.

At the beginning of the next month I sidled into Martha's office one afternoon after lunch, before staff meeting.

"Hey, Marth, are you up for a little visit to Julie's? We owe her a call. I told her we'd be dropping in on her to see how she'd spent her food stamps."

Martha gave me one of those inside, knowing glances, stashed her pocketbook, and picked up a sweater. We stuck our heads into Smitty's office to tell him where we'd be and that we'd be back shortly. He just laughed, and we went down the stairs and told Dorothy at the desk that we'd be back in about half an hour or so.

The apartment was decent enough. It had lots of big windows, was bright, and with Wallace in charge it was tidy and cleaned up. It had a rug on the floor, a few toys, and a bit of furniture—a plaid couch and a real crib. Julie was not pleased to see us. We reminded her why we were there and made our way, past Wallace's drinking buddies, who mostly ignored us, to the kitchen area in back.

Julie opened the refrigerator door. There was a package of

oxtails, a jar of extra-fancy olives, a package of bologna, a carton of orange juice, and some other items—about eleven dollars' worth in all. She had about three dollars' worth of food stamps left, and it was the day after they had arrived. She had twenty-nine days to go until the next stamps would arrive.

She could tell us nothing. Did she understand? Did she really get it? Was she at all capable of managing? She could not manage alone, but neither could she seem to find a person to live with who was not an alcoholic. She invariably turned over her stamps, then turned to the food pantries. Between the pantries and the on-site meal programs, no one was starving, but no one was thriving, either. We left.

At the staff meeting we shared the dilemma with the staff—the teachers, clergy, and business manager. What did they think? Suggestions?

In the end we decided that each of us would put Julie on our prayer lists. We also had a newsletter, and we decided that we would write up the story and problems of this woman, ask our wider Christian community to pray about Julie, Emily, and Terence, and if anyone had any suggestions or inspiration, to please get in touch with us.

Meanwhile I called Diane, her new caseworker at ICH&A, and gave her the update on the children and the newest address, plus the information that the children were now in the preschool program. Then I went to the file to document, document, document.

John

Ruth, our learning center teacher and worship coordinator, was laughing in her alto voice, with her green eyes sparkling and her face melting. "Lynn, when I was here yesterday for worship there was a call for you on the answering machine. It was from John. He's at the VA hospital. He said to tell you that he's had a hysterectomy and wants you to visit him." Ruth continued to laugh in her easy, laid-back way, and we tried to think of words that might possibly sound like hysterectomy to mean what had happened to John. We couldn't think of a thing.

It was Monday and a food day, and there would be a staff meeting at one o'clock, so today would not be a good day to go downtown. Tomorrow was a visiting day and paperwork day for me. I would plan to visit John then. I called the VA hospital to get the visiting hours and leaned back to reflect some on John. Oh, John. Poor John. Dear John.

I recalled so many incidents—snatched bits of conversation here and there, arguments, tirades, bashful fence-mending. Once in the early years, when I had met John on the street and told him to come to the office to pick out some clothes and he hadn't, I had hunted him up. He was living on the top floor of a five-story walk-up building on Lawrence Avenue, and as I left the office to walk the block and a half to John's, I called back over my shoulder to tell folks where I was going and headed out.

As I turned east on Lawrence at the light, then crossed to the south side of the street, I noticed a group of men congregated halfway down the block. It was the kind of group that hung together to pass drugs or to share a bottle or some kind of trouble. Heads were down in a huddle, not eye to eye in the easy conversation of pals. If the men were high, their behavior would be unreliable. My general rule of thumb for walking the street safely was to cross to the other side when huddled groups occupied the center lane of the sidewalk. I thought to myself, Where is John's building? Is it before or after these thugs? If I don't come to his building first, will I cross over? or pass them? Is it tempting fate? Is it foolhardy? I've got kids at home who are my primary responsibility!

I arrived at 905 Lawrence Avenue before coming abreast of the men, so I turned in, relieved, but only briefly. This was not a security building—no buzzer system here. One just walked in. I knew the men had seen me, had been eyeing my journey to 905, and once in the building and on my way up the stairs, I had fears of their coming after me. I got to the top floor and realized that the only way down was the way I had come up, that I was trapped. I could feel my heart beating in my throat and prayed to God that John was home.

I knocked on the door, heard the slightest rustling, and knocked again. A sleepy, bored voice said, "Yeah?" and I said, "John, hi. It's Lynn. Open up."

"What? Is that you, Mrs. Perry? How could that be?"

"Yeah, John, it's me," I answered. "Come on, open the door."

"I must be dreaming," he continued to ramble. "Why would Mrs. Perry come to see me? What have I done? It must be my imagination. It can't be that Mrs. Perry would come here!"

"John, you've died and gone to heaven. Now open the door!"

A deferential and pompous John opened the door, bowed deeply, and said, "Come in, Mrs. Perry, welcome to my humble dwelling. And would you like to have a cup of coffee or something?"

I explained that I had come to escort him to the office to assist him with finding some clothes, encouraged him to get his shoes on in a hurry, and agreed to wait inside the doorway. No three-year-old could have made a longer production of getting shoes on than John did that afternoon. I was anxious about the men on the street, anxious about John's imagination regarding my being at his place, and eager to head back to the office. When we finally got down to the street, the men had gone, and I was relieved.

Other visits with John flooded my memory. He would often, even after many years, call me Linda. I would say, "John, my name is Lynn. Just plain Lynn." He'd fly into a rage. "Well, pardon me,

Mrs. Perry, I know you're a married woman . . ." and we'd be off and running, and John would stalk out of the office, furious. On his return, usually within the week, he'd have a small box of candy, or a card, or a humble apology. Time to smoke the peace pipe, which usually generated another war, because he would take my hand, kiss my hand, then to my horror begin to move up my arm. And when I pulled back, he'd be yelling again. It seemed impossible to get it right. There seemed to be no way to strike a balance with John. I liked him. He had such a rough life. I didn't want to appear seductive or playful with him—it wasn't fair. Yet I wanted him to feel cared about. He was too needy, though, and so desperately lonely that hello was too much, it seemed. I'd get distressed enough by his behavior that I'd wind up screaming and yelling too and know that I'd lost it. I wasn't any more dispassionate than he was, though our aims were different.

Poor John. Memories of his broad, smiling face came to mind as I rode the Sheridan bus downtown in midday. I got off at Huron Street and walked east to the VA hospital. It was enormous. I'd never been in this hospital before, and it was a different animal than the local hospitals. It wasn't plushy—no carpets, no gift shops, no phone-in-every-room courtesies or TV-in-every-room individual treatments. It was military style—group TV in the room at the end of the hall and a pay phone on the wall. Patients looked like victims of war, and the bodies that manned the wheelchairs were more mangled than the average population sample.

I inquired at the enormous reception desk for John's room number and took the elevator to the floor as directed. I gave my name at the nurse's station and asked how John was doing; the nurse pointed me in the direction of his room.

John was delighted with company, and we had a wonderful visit. John, cleaned up and dried out, was a sight. He looked great and sounded pretty normal. He began to talk about being there, then about his hysterectomy.

"John," I said, "I don't know what they did to you—there are many possibilities—but I can promise you that you haven't had a hysterectomy!"

"Then what's this doughnut?" he said, whipping his gown up over his shoulder and pointing to a round object that resembled a doughnut and was located at waist level. I closed my eyes and leaned back a bit as John lowered his gown. John's information was vague, and patient confidentiality was such that finding out exactly what had happened might be difficult, but it appeared they had performed a temporary procedure following treatment for a bowel obstruction or even removal of part of the intestine due to a blockage or possible cancer.

We continued the good visit, and when I left I promised to return. I visited John on a regular basis, every Tuesday or every other Tuesday, and it was fun. John was so much better than he'd been in years. The prolonged separation from alcohol did wonders for his temperament and his memory, and the nourishment of food instead of booze put color in his cheeks, a bit of flesh on his arms, and a spring that spelled recovery in his gait. His handshake was very strong—viselike, in fact—and he seemed to be a pet of the nurses and social work staff.

When his birthday rolled around, I baked a cake to take on my visit—something he could have for himself and something to share with other patients and staff people who visited him in his room. He was pleased, and I wondered if he'd ever before in his whole life had a birthday cake.

One day I arrived wearing green. It's my favorite color, and I had a green jumper and a white blouse with green shamrocks on it. It was a good thing to wear while visiting a big Irishman. I had just settled in when the Catholic chaplain, Father Hanlon, dropped by. John introduced us. "Father, this is the woman I told you about, the one who baked me the birthday cake. She comes to see me all the time—I don't know why," he said, smiling. The priest was friendly and gracious, and asked John if he'd like Communion. "Yes, Father," he said, and they indicated that I should stay.

"John has made a good confession," Father Hanlon said to me, dipping his head and half genuflecting. I took that to mean that John had told the priest about the man he had murdered so many years before.

I sat in an armchair in that very tiny private room. There was one hospital bed, one bedside stand, a floor lamp, a metal wardrobe, and the chair I sat in. The room was the size of a closet. The items were squeezed in. There was space for a doctor, nurse, priest, or visitor to walk in and stand on one side of the bed only, as the bed was lengthwise against the wall, but the room was not big enough for much else.

Father Hanlon put on his stole, opened his breviary, placed the elements on the over-bed table, and began, "The Lord be with you," and John responded, "And with thy spirit." John had responded—miracles do happen. Liturgy—the words of our childhood, the words of our youth. Each of us has a liturgy, and it can be summoned up after years of stagnation and disuse to bring healing. John hadn't been to mass in thirty years, yet here he was, at middle age, and the Christ within John was assisting him to reach back and claim the wholeness promised—nothing less than the very body of Christ.

Angelo and
Jackie Raino

*O*h, no, it's crazy Maxine," was the weary statement of a coworker. Maxine had come for food but had gravitated to another staff person. She wasn't my sheep. I recognized her, heard vague references to her behavior in passing and more specific details in a staff meeting. I hadn't spoken with her beyond a hello but had absorbed a few things about her superficially. She had three children—a quiet, fearful-looking boy named Roger, a bouncy, red-haired lump with curls named Mandy, and a baby. Maxine was pregnant. There were allusions to a mystical, magical belief system, but I paid little attention. I was too absorbed by the concerns of my own people.

The Ministry preschool met on Tuesdays and Thursdays, and one day I wandered in to get some supplies from the storage closet. I stopped to sit on the floor to talk with some of the children and giggle with them, and while doing this was drawn toward the infant on a blanket. I love to hold babies, and my hands itched to cuddle him, so I reached down to pick up the warm, tiny Angelo. He was five months old, but had been a preemie, and so he weighed only twelve pounds. The expected thing about holding babies is the way they curve around to fit in the cradle of one's arms. Angelo did not. Angelo just lay sprawled in my arms. It seemed impossible to tuck in what felt like five arms and legs. He did not snuggle, did not curl, did not fit. This baby did not know how to be held.

I became alert. I now paid attention. Something was very wrong here. I began to hear more and make note of more details about this situation. The mother talked to Reverend Tom about the baby. She referred to the baby as evil. The child cried at home all the time, and the mother refused to pick him up, believing he was an evil baby.

Information about the older children began to come through.

The little boy, Roger, might be retarded. In a deprived environment this is often difficult to recognize. A child who is not spoken to often does not bother to talk. A child who receives no intellectual stimulation through toys, books, or conversation does not reflect much understanding. The challenge was to provide warm, interesting activities during preschool so that Roger would begin to develop.

Mandy had demonstrated a dramatic change. She had not talked or even moved around very much when she began with the preschool program, but was soon running and playing, laughing, talking, and experimenting with toilet training. Growth! Such a natural process it is, but still miraculous.

The Ministry was blessed with many wonderful volunteers. The preschool volunteer was Jackie, and this story is really about Jackie. She would say that it was about Angelo, because Jackie loved Angelo, but it's about Jackie, because it's a love story, and Jackie is the lover.

Jackie was an RN—blond, dainty, effervescent, and full of fun. At the time when Angelo came into her life, Jackie had been married for twenty-five years, had three beautiful daughters, a handsome and successful husband, and a fine house in an affluent suburb. Jackie hadn't been employed since she was married, except as a special-duty nurse for friends or family members who were sick.

Jackie's first contact with The Ministry came about through her children. School friends of theirs were collecting food and Christmas items through their church for poor families in Uptown. Even though Jackie and her family were not members of that church, they were drawn to the project and signed up to provide for a family at Christmas. They got the list with names of the children and their sizes and ages, and delivered a Christmas tree with all the decorations, a turkey dinner with all the trimmings, clothing and toys for the children, and things for the mother and father. Jackie's family was always available for holiday donations, then they began to visit, and eventually Jackie responded to a call for a volunteer to help in the parent/child preschool program.

When the first teachers, Ruth and Jan, began work at The Ministry, they planned an after-school program for teens. They soon found that teens were not in school—they had long since dropped out in this area of town, so the women readjusted their Learning Center program to junior high children. They found that even that age was late. The children were missing so many skills that even though they maintained the program for their age group, Ruth and Jan continued to develop programs for younger and younger children until they were working with preschool children. Once at that point, they discovered that even preschool was not young enough, because the parents of the preschoolers, most often single mothers, had had such a deprived upbringing themselves that they didn't know how to parent. Thus was born the parent/child preschool program. The program met two mornings per week, and while the children were in the learning center the parents met on one morning to do an activity—a craft or something with nutrition or something that they had asked to learn—and on the other morning they had a sharing time plus aid with parenting techniques.

When Maxine's children became part of the preschool program, this multifaceted network became part of Maxine's support system, along with the food pantry resources and counseling services.

One Tuesday, Maxine called to say that she had a bad cold and couldn't get the children to preschool. Jackie arranged to pick them up. Maxine lived on our block, way down at the other end, so it was not a great difficulty to get the children. Jackie made two trips, one walking while holding the two older children by the hand, then going back for the baby. When preschool was over for the morning the baby was sleeping, so Jackie left Angelo sleeping in the preschool room with Jan and walked the older children home first. When she returned she said, "You know, Maxine is really very sick. I can't imagine how she can possibly take care of that baby. What would you think if I asked her if I could take the baby home with me? Do you think I should? I'm really worried about the baby with a mother that sick."

Jackie returned to Maxine's house to ask her, and arrived back at The Ministry with a few items of clothing and wide eyes. "May I use your phone? I have to call home and see what my kids can rustle up! Maxine said I can take the baby home with me!"

Jackie took the baby home, and the novelty was quite wonderful for her family. The following Thursday, Jackie and Angelo were back, and Jackie went to get Roger and Mandy for preschool. At the end of the morning, as baby Angelo was sleeping again, Jackie walked the older children home first. I didn't work in the preschool, but I had a vague sense of the comings and goings, the vehicles in the driveway, the shifts in the building sounds, doors opening and closing, and children's voices (and cries). It had quieted down. It was the quiet that alerted me to the running on the stairs. I looked up and it was Jackie, running into my office. I got up from my chair at the urgency in the air and walked around my desk to have Jackie fall into my arms, crying.

"Lynn, that woman gave me her baby! Look, here's the birth certificate! How can you give your baby away?" The afternoon was spent on the phone with the Illinois Department of Children and Family Services (IDCFS) to arrange emergency foster home placement for Angelo and to have the process begun for Jackie to be certified.

Jackie thought, as a nurse, that something was not right with Angelo. Following a week with Jackie and her family, and as soon as all the paperwork was in place, Angelo was admitted to the hospital for tests and an evaluation. The excessive crying seemed to be the result of seizures that the baby had been having, and he was placed on anticonvulsive medication. When his condition had been stabilized, Jackie was allowed to take him home again. The intervening week had given the family a space of time to adjust to having a baby in the house. The first week had been a lark, but the family was now about to settle in for the long haul.

Thanksgiving came, and Christmas, and Jackie brought in reports of the family's adjustment to having a baby in the house. There were all the clothes and the change of schedules and the equipment! Jackie thought that probably most interesting were the reactions of her daughters' friends, especially the boys. Who's the baby? Where's the mother? What about the father? It was an educational opportunity about responsible parenthood, with the not-too-hard-to-draw conclusions about responsible sex. Jackie had to say very little. The baby, Angelo, the rejected and unwanted child, spoke volumes.

The IDCFS had wheels turning in the search for an adoptive home for Angelo. Maxine had agreed to sign papers to terminate her parental rights. During this time, Maxine decided to take her two remaining children and return to her parents out of state. That was good news. It meant that Maxine would receive some emotional support and supervision, and that Roger and Mandy would receive additional nurturing as part of an extended family. It also meant that Maxine would be less likely to renege on final arrangements to relinquish Angelo for adoption.

Maxine's bus out of town was one day after her lease was up, but she had to stay until that day to receive her last welfare check. It meant that her final night in Uptown she spent sleeping on the couch at The Ministry. A staff person sat guard over her to keep her from leaving and upsetting all these careful plans, and also because of her tendency to wake up screaming about demons.

In the spring, on Good Friday, the adoptive parents came to Jackie's home to collect baby Angelo. Angelo had lived with Jackie and her family for four and a half months, and Jackie said that if it had been one week longer, she never could have surrendered the baby. Jackie gave Angelo a silver cup. She thought it would be important, she said, for Angelo to know that even before his adoptive parents had him, he had lived with people who loved him.

Julie

*B*ut what do I know about this, really? What right do I have to say that this is bad—or dangerous—for Julie's children? Who am I to make such a judgment? I'm just a plain person—a housewife!" I was on the phone with a caseworker from the Illinois Department of Children and Family Services (IDCFS), and my doubts were showing.

"Now look here, Lynn, you're a mother, you've been around, and you've seen a lot of unusual things where you work. When one person stands out even in that situation, of course you know it's not normal."

I finally decided to concentrate my energy on removing the children from the home. I would be the advocate for the children.

Julie had become restless. She no longer stayed with someone for several months before moving on. Now she would be only weeks with a man. When he would drink and become violent, she would move again. It was hard to find her. She didn't keep appointments at the preschool, and she had long since given up even talking about seeing her baby, Jill, or keeping an appointment to see her. She had finally terminated her parental rights for Jill.

One afternoon, while out in the neighborhood making home visits, Martha and I met Julie sauntering down the street carrying a big box of food. "Julie, where did you get that stuff?" we asked, amazed.

"Oh, I got it from St. Augustine's. For Wallace." St. Augustine's was an Episcopal church and drop-in center with a specific mission to the Native American community in Uptown. That Julie was not a Native American and did not even live in their geographic area but still had gotten food from the center was an indication of who Julie was: Everyone knew her, she always needed something, and it was impossible for her to comply with any requests or regulations.

In early April, Julie was staying in Wallace's apartment while he was in the hospital. He would not allow her to have the key—she had to get the building manager to let her in as she came and went, but she had a place to stay. Terence was with her, but not Emily.

"Julie, where's Emily? Why don't you have her?" I asked, more than a little curious.

"How can I when Jeff won't let me take her? Why should I go back there when Jeff gave me a black eye?" Julie whined. Jeff had kicked Julie out. He had taken her clothes and Terence's clothes. He'd held Terence upside down by one foot and beaten him and called him a nigger, Julie reported. Jeff was drinking heavily again.

For two straight days Julie and I talked about what it could mean if she could have a breather—get herself together, perhaps have surgery for her incontinence, work on her weight, find a decent place to live, get settled and stabilized. The wear and tear were really showing on her—she flew into rages easily and cried at the drop of a hat. She came around to the idea that a break would be good for her and agreed to call IDCFS to ask for placement for her children.

Quite satisfied with myself and hardly daring to experience the thrill of relief, I dialed the number and gave Julie the phone. In no time she was screaming and yelling and carrying on about how she would never give up the children, would never turn them over to the state—and a room full of blue air followed.

I got on the phone, hoping to sort out the confusion of misunderstandings. The caseworker very simply said, "We are not taking any voluntaries."

"What? How can you say that? I've been working for days to get this woman to agree to this, I've been documenting and following her for years, and finally—finally she agrees to place her children. And you tell me that you can't take them?" I was furious.

"You don't understand," she said calmly. "If we take a voluntary, we can do hours of paperwork and phone calls and make all kinds of arrangements and still have no power because the mother has not agreed to termination of parental rights. We're just a babysitter for her. All she has to do is snap her fingers and she gets the children back because she retains custody—we don't have it. We can't afford that time. You get her to surrender her parental rights and give the state custody, and we'll take the children. But no way are we doing this."

I had not been polite, and now I was so discouraged, felt so stupid, and understood so well the problems that the caseworker had described. I just wished I had understood a little better before the phone call. Voluntary had two meanings to the caseworker: I had understood only one, "voluntary placement." The voluntary that the caseworker was seeking was "voluntary surrender of parental rights." I had needlessly harassed a lot of people without understanding all the terminology about guardianship, only thinking I understood. Now I had to calm down a very wild and raving Julie. A solution seemed further away than when I had begun.

Wallace returned from the hospital and agreed to keep Terence, but Julie had to stay with friends in an apartment upstairs—Wallace refused to have her living with him.

Now Julie was really determined to get Emily back from Jeff. Since Julie was the mother, and we had a copy of Emily's birth certificate without Jeff's name on it, it seemed reasonable that Julie should be able to get Emily. We called the police and went over to Jeff's in a squad car. Doing so took a fair amount of courage, since he had threatened to kill Julie if she ever came after him with the police, and he said that after killing her he would take Emily and get out of state. But there was no Jeff. He was not home, nor was he at the home of Emily's usual babysitter.

After a weekend of rest I was reenergized enough to try again. I also had learned a few things that were to prove helpful. For instance, I now knew that being "undomiciled," as IDCFS called it, was enough to warrant immediate intervention. Basically at this point Julie was undomiciled. She did not have her own address. In order to receive welfare, a person was required to have an address. Technically, she was putting her status in jeopardy. Without an address, she would have no need for rent money from her welfare check.

Julie came in for food on Wednesday. Wallace was back in the hospital for some follow-up, and Julie was staying at his apartment, but she wanted food and she wanted Emily. Right now, thank you very much.

Instead of calling the regional office, I called the main IDCFS office downtown and spoke about the case with the assistant administrator, who said that first they needed to find out if it was an active case. I was told that someone would get back to me. After giving Julie food, I asked her to wait downstairs, but she was impatient and insisted that she had to get back to the apartment to give Terence a nap. She wasn't going to hang around. I acceded to this request and told her that I would come over if I found out anything.

The call from IDCFS came in after one o'clock. They had done all the checking and, yes, it was an active case. Bingo! "I want those kids," the assistant administrator told me. "You get that little girl out of Jeff's place. The way to do it is to call the police and ask for a juvenile officer, not beat cops. If you can't get the little girl, don't place the one kid. Wait until you get them both."

When I went over to the Sheridan Road building where Wallace's apartment was, I climbed the stairs to the second floor after being buzzed in. I turned right and was planning to head toward Wallace's apartment when I saw Julie wandering around the hall in the opposite direction. Terence was with her. It seemed that Julie had begun to fix lunch, then wandered down the hall to see a friend. Terence had followed her out of the apartment, and when he closed the door behind him, it locked. The building manager was away from the building, and Julie was therefore locked out. Now she was really "undomiciled."

"Come on, Julie, let's go over to The Ministry and see if we can do something about getting Emily," I said, and she followed me down the stairs. Terence had no shoes on. It was a chilly Chicago day, April 19, sunny and bright, but windy. I unzipped the green down jacket I was wearing and tucked Terence inside, holding his legs around my waist to keep his feet protected. I hustled down Sheridan Road the short distance to Lakeside and hurried up the steps to our building, shielding Terence's head from the cold in the chilly wind. I put him down and took off my coat. Then I called the police station, got the juvenile division, and requested assistance.

The officer who arrived looked like a movie star—slim, cute, strawberry-blond curly hair—and she drove a "blue and white," a city of Chicago squad car.

After I explained the situation, the officer left. She called from Jeff's apartment to say that he was not there. The landlady let her into the apartment, and it was very clean, she said—everything was tidy. She would try the building where the woman lived who baby-sat for Emily when Jeff was working.

The officer got to the building, knocked on the door, and asked for Emily. The woman looked at the police officer, opened the door wide, stood back out of the way, and said, "Here's the father—ask him yourself."

We were watching from one of the front windows when I saw the police officer walking up the street holding Emily's hand. I couldn't believe it. She entered the building, and we all went upstairs with the children. I went to call IDCFS. When I had spoken with the assistant administrator earlier, she told me that if I got the children I should call the IDCFS hotline. "When you get those kids," she said, "and you want to place them, you call the hotline. I will advise all the phone operators and the supervisors that we are working on a placement for those kids right now. You ask for the supervisor and you say that this is an emergency. You will get through."

I called and got through. I was asked if I had both children, and I said yes. I told them the boy was with the mother, and they were both here at the building. When I had arrived at our building carrying Terence, everyone had said, "Let's clean Terence up a bit— let's find him shoes," but I said, "No. We'll send him just like that. You leave him dirty. You leave his shoes off. This is the way his mother cares for him."

Julie came upstairs. Then the police officer came upstairs. She said, "The mother has been informed that the children are not going home."

Julie cried a bit and said, "I thought I could have them for a couple of hours. I'd like to take them to St. Thomas's Church tonight for the spaghetti supper."

My head started to spin, wondering how to figure this out. We were so close. Princess Red Feather, our community volunteer who distributed clothing, was just coming out of the clothing room. "Princess Red Feather," I said, "are you going to St. Thomas's for supper tonight?" At her nod, I rushed on, "Could Julie go along with you?" Red Feather smiled, then Julie smiled, and they linked arms and headed for the door.

Smitty, Reverend Tom, and Martha were open-mouthed. The

only glitch now was that IDCFS had no available transportation, but Tom agreed to drive the children to the downtown office. We grabbed two blankets out of the closet, found some stuffed animals, and packed them into the car with the children. We stood on the sidewalk and watched them all leave—Terence and Emily in the back of Tom's old blue car, packed into the back seat like little peas, and Julie and Red Feather, walking arm in arm down the street on the way to St. Thomas and carrying a box—something for Julie to give away, no doubt.

Beth

*J*an had taken the simple pre-
school idea, begun as a volunteer project, and turned it into a Cad-
illac of a program. Renamed the Parent-Child Preschool Program,
it was unique and innovative.

Jan enlisted the aid of most of the staff and a good many volunteers. For many children in Uptown, even though the family situation might be dreadful, one point in their favor was that those
children had been loved and hugged and held and read to by many
social workers, clergymen, teachers, and loving volunteers. Jan
worked with the children, and on Tuesday Reverend Tom assisted
her. On Thursday, Jackie Raino was the helper. In addition to his
duties with the food pantry, Richard drove the van and collected
the parents and children who traveled from any distance of more
than a city block. Different volunteers did crafts or cooking projects. Our other teacher, Ruth, often taught nutrition segments, and
for a time, I did a class in needlepoint.

When Jan suggested the idea, I had misgivings: Needlepoint is
something that movie stars do while they wait on the set. Rosie
Grier does needlepoint. I think of it as an aristocratic craft—it's
fairly expensive, picky, and time-consuming—but I was game.
After all, for me it would be like having a day off, playing at work.

First came the process of gathering all the stuff—eight rulers,
eight needles, eight twelve-inch squares of canvas bound on the
edges with masking tape, eight thimbles, and a large assortment of
yarn. I sifted through my books and chose an assortment of pretty
stitches, drew some graphs and large diagrams with directions, and
dittoed off a batch of little booklets. Two women who were not
in the mothers' group, but were interested in needlepoint, asked
permission to join our sessions.

Beth was one of the mothers. She was small, about five feet tall without shoes, slight of build, with blue eyes and a lot of coarse blond hair, dark at the roots. The proportion of hair to body was reminiscent of Sparkle Plenty, the cartoon character. Beth had a very deep voice and she was quite hyper. She vibrated when she talked, and she had difficulty sitting still. She had a nervous laugh and a peculiar bass register, and her eyes had the filmy glaze of medication. When Richard stopped at Beth's with the van, he often had to wait because Beth was not ready. It was not only that she was not ready—she could not get ready. Her four-year-old son Donald, whom she called Prince, might be dressed, but if so he had probably been dressed by Beth's husband Donnie, or by Noel, Beth's ten-year-old daughter. Noel was Beth's daughter by another man, and this girl was a gem. While Beth would jump around, saying she couldn't find things or didn't know what to do, Noel would calmly dress her mother, gather purse, apartment key, and Prince, and organize the family into the waiting van. I would see Noel with her mother and think of a sad reinterpretation of Wordsworth's famous line: "the Child is father of the Man."

Now Beth, who couldn't seem to tie her own shoes, was going to do needlepoint. Fat chance.

The women gathered. I passed out the supplies, showed a few things that I had done, plus some samples of the stitches and how they looked, and attempted to teach each woman a basic stitch. The stitch was really quite simple, but it was not a surprise that Beth could not do it. No one was more eager, however. She clutched the canvas, crossed her legs, bent over the work, and went at it with zeal. Hovering, I would make little suggestions, just enough not to be discouraging but expecting nothing. Beth requested a rather large piece of canvas and left with needle, thimble, directions, and a hunk of yarn.

I was surprised that she returned the next week, as the women had the option of a cooking session. But when she pulled her work out of a bag, surprise gave way to awe. She had a piece of canvas twelve inches wide and fifteen inches long. She had stitched the names of members of her family on the canvas and had filled in the spaces with an elaborate stitch. It was a genuine needlepoint stitch—not one of the assortment listed in the booklet, but one she had concocted in her attempts to do a simpler stitch. Not only had she been working on this, but it was already half finished. Not only was it half finished but she had bought some yarn herself, and the color choices, a combination that I would never have chosen or thought of, were dazzling. I was stunned. I sputtered and shook my head, and she laughed and laughed. Maybe she couldn't tie her shoes, but she was a gifted needleworker. To accomplish the amount of stitching that she had done, she must have worked day and night. I was fascinated.

The next week she returned with the finished item and wanted more canvas. I unrolled the mesh and cut a similar piece for her, letting her tape the raw edge herself. It was heartwarming to see how people responded to her work. The other women were impressed as Beth proudly but shyly showed her work. The staff people would look benignly at Beth as she walked up to them, and they would smile a bland smile until they saw the canvas. Then, to a person, their eyes would pop open and they'd look at the canvas then look quickly at me. I'd nod the unspoken yes, that it really was Beth's work, and Beth would laugh and jump up and down in the knowledge of a triumph. It was super.

The following week she was back with another canvas, half finished—this time with the names of people on Donnie's side of the family. She finished that piece as rapidly as the first and wanted more canvas. People remarked about how alert Beth had become. It was a new kind of therapy! The next week when she returned, she carefully unrolled her canvas, and there was a little boy. I looked at her, wondering, and she said, "Donnie drew him for me." She began to stitch away at the little body and the blue shorts.

Beth knew she had me now, and the next week she strode in and, laughing out loud, unrolled the canvas on the desk and stood back with her hands behind her back, looking victorious. I smiled and hugged her. She giggled in her deep throaty giggle and asked for more canvas. I was reminded of the story of the elves and the shoemaker—no sooner were new supplies laid out than the projects were speedily completed.

Over the next few months Beth finished about eight canvases, each one more beautiful than the former. The most unusual thing to me about her work was her use of color. If I were doing a child with a wagon, there would have been blue sky and green grass—

very traditional. Beth's use of color was extraordinary, and it crea-
ted a new heaven and a new earth that was dramatic and striking.
The picture of the little boy had a yellow sky with shades of pink
and peach in the foreground. Looking at her work changed the
way I saw space. She did not use the primary colors, but instead
those colors tucked between the blends in the spectrum—a soft
rainbow, bursting with light.

Beth was like Ray and so many others Reverend Mick meant
when he used to talk about what he called "grace for the moment"
people. In needlepoint class Beth was more than together and with
it—she was the teacher's teacher. Seeing this poor woman creating
new rainbows of color filled me with euphoria, and I could feel my
heart leap within me at the sight of Beth's creation. As Wordsworth said,

> My heart leaps up when I behold
>   A rainbow in the sky:
> So was it when my life began;
> So is it now I am a man;
> So be it when I shall grow old,
>   Or let me die!
> The Child is father of the Man;
> And I could wish my days to be
> Bound each to each by natural piety.*

*William Wordsworth, "My Heart Leaps Up When I Behold," *The Poetical Works
of William Wordsworth*, vol. 1 (London: Edward Moxon, 1857), 166.

Gloria

$\mathcal{T}$he first time Gloria came to The Ministry, she had been referred by an agency called Aid to Alcoholics. She had run short of groceries, so she signed up to get food from our food pantry. A staff member, in a conversation with Gloria, invited her to join in a sharing group with some of the other community people who gathered to talk about the issues in their lives—poverty, safety in the neighborhood and the buildings where they lived, fears of illness, what to do when someone steals your shoes, loneliness, powerlessness, and sorrow.

My instant reaction to Gloria was intense dislike. She was very fat, had short, curly red hair, skinny legs with a toeing-out, cramped walk, an enormous beer belly and red nose (probably a result of heavy drinking), and a mannish voice that boasted tactlessly about her strong opinions. She never smiled. During the months in which the sharing group met, there was an open invitation to Bible class—not unusual since we were a church organization. Gloria made it clear that she had no interest in any such plan. She resented her strict religious upbringing and would have no part in such goings-on. Fine, Gloria. Sit in your enormous lump of yourself and just be. No one is going to bug you here.

Gloria disappeared for a while and then resurfaced. She had had a slip—another round of drinking—but she would not admit it. It is a difficult line for the caregiver to walk: When does acceptance mean to ignore a problem? And when does acceptance require one to confront the other? Gloria bore the unmistakeable signs of a drinking bout, but she denied drinking. Other folks on the street reported that Gloria had been hard at it, but none of the staff had seen it firsthand. Certain of the people we served took great delight in informing us about a weak sister or brother who was drunk, in which tavern, when and with whom. This information was not necessarily reliable, either. Were the people friends, or were they in competition with one another? Was the informant drunk or sober at the time? Was the informant envious of staff concern for the other? The buildings that sheltered microcosms of grand, supportive communities also had knots of mean-spiritedness and minor treachery.

Gloria did her disappearing act frequently through the next year, and then suddenly she stuck like glue. She had a companion named Pete, who lived in her building. Gloria was a very private woman, a "one friend at a time" person. Her current friend was Pete. They each had a "one room with a hot plate and a bath down the hall" apartment, and they spent time together constantly. They ate in the evening at Pete's; they had lunch at Gloria's. They fed Pete's dog.

We never met Pete, but one cold day in February, Gloria found him dead. Gloria parked herself at our office and became a pet of the whole staff. We referred to her as a person of hope. We spoke about her when we gave talks at churches that supported our work. One women's group responded by sending money for Gloria—ten dollars a month on a regular basis for her to have some "extras." When the staff member who had made the contact told Gloria the good news and asked if that would help her in her limited circumstances, she said that fifteen would be better.

The money did help Gloria, and because of it she no longer needed to come to our food pantry toward the end of the month when her food stamps ran out. It seemed on the surface that Gloria was "making it," but there was strong disagreement among staff members. "Gloria isn't here because the money has given her enough to drink on" was one opinion. That point of view, along with those who maintained it, was held in strong contempt by others on the staff, who accused the first of being skeptical and not having trust in people. The skeptics called the others dreamers and unrealistic people who did not face facts.

Gloria would arrive on the fifteenth of every month to collect her money. She was dry, if not sober, but the arguments among staff people raged on. The glue had loosened, and we saw little of Gloria.

One day she came for her money and had to wait around the

office for a while, so she came to talk with me. It was quiet that day, and she began to unfold herself—relax in a chair and share with me some of her history. It was the first peek inside Gloria that I had ever had.

She had been adopted when she was sixteen months old by an older, very strict couple. The demands placed on her by her mother were severe enough that she left home as soon as she was old enough and took a job in Chicago's Loop. She worked as an elevator operator in the days when all elevators had operators and all operators wore white gloves. The strain was more than she could bear. She was nervous when the elevator was empty and nervous when there were people on it. People got on, Gloria grew tense. People got off, Gloria grew tense.

Toward the close of World War II, when the city was teeming with young men in uniform, Gloria found that she was less tense with a certain young sailor, so they went to city hall and got married. The way the young sailor "stayed loose," as Gloria said, was to drink heavily and beat her. The marriage lasted for about a month and a half. Then Gloria left. She wound up in California, had a nervous breakdown, and spent three and a half years in a mental hospital. She eventually returned to the Midwest, and the person we knew was the product of a toughness that did not tone the muscle, but broke the spirit. Gloria was a frightened, nervous, angry, distrustful, and sad woman. Finally, I had seen some of that person. I still did not like her very much, but I had crossed the line to having some feeling for her—if only pity. It was my problem, and I felt guilty about it, but she was hard to warm to.

One spring day, after about a four-year relationship with Gloria, several staff people commented about the same time that Gloria hadn't been around for a while. Reverend Tom decided to go check her out and didn't return for hours. When he arrived at Gloria's room, he found her in a diabetic coma. He called an ambulance, and she was taken to the nearest hospital. The following day she had a heart attack and remained in the hospital for three months.

The next time Gloria walked in to see us, she was indeed a new creation. She was a woman thirty pounds lighter, minus her pack of cigarettes. She carried a can of diet soda in one pocket and a small jar of decaffeinated coffee in the other. Gloria was stone-cold sober. She was grateful to Tom and so amazed to be alive that she was humble and awestruck.

The Ministry had been of as little account to Gloria as a Band-Aid, but now she was really aware that we had something to do with healing. What had been only a superficial attachment to The Ministry had given way to Christian community; Gloria was one of our people—a real sheep in the fold. Our relationship was now mutual. "I just dropped by to say hello," or "Jan was sick yesterday. Is she better?" or "Would you like me to put these letters in the mailbox?" She hung around, she went out, she came in, but we were community, and Gloria belonged. She attended worship and Bible class and was more relaxed.

After a year of balance, disaster hit Gloria again. She wandered over to our office in a paper dress to see Reverend Jim. Gloria's building had been destroyed by fire; all her meager belongings were damaged by smoke and water, and her paper dress had been issued by the Red Cross. It was March, a cold Chicago March, and Gloria was frozen. "I had to come here—I had no place else to go." Gloria was given clothing, comfort, and a place from which to call her mother, with whom she had a Christmas-card and disaster-only dialogue.

She was given shelter, and then relocated. Things again returned to normal, and Gloria continued to drop by daily and to come for any activity that was going on. She came earlier and earlier and earlier. Gloria was camped on our doorstep when we opened at eight in the morning. Gloria was a pest. She came to see Reverend Jim or Jan, and they were infinitely patient. I marveled at their warmth.

Every so often there's an item in the paper, usually from another city, or it appears as a tag item at the end of the evening news, describing the bizarre lifestyle of some recluse who had shoeboxes filled with cash, or was found several days dead in the back room of a home stacked floor to ceiling with newspapers. One of these items hit the front page of Chicago's daily papers. It reported the death of an old woman in a house filled with eighty-some cats. The woman was a wealthy widow, and she lived on the west side of the city. The Board of Health went to the home and declared it unfit, and the Humane Society came with trucks and workers to round up the cats, many of whom were sick. It was awful. The woman was also Gloria's mother.

As the only heir, the legacy of this home could have meant a new life for Gloria: She could have sold it and lived modestly in a smaller home or put the money in savings and continued to live in an apartment. She could have done many things, or rather, there were many options, but they were not options for a person such as Gloria. Gloria was too wounded, had too many scars. The life Gloria had led not only had harmed her, but had erased some skills. Her coping ability was greatly diminished, and the very idea of having any money or having to make decisions made Gloria so tense she could hardly talk. Instead she came to the office with forms to fill out to waive all rights to her inheritance. She chose to continue with her small SSI allotment and her monthly food stamps. With time Gloria relaxed again. All paperwork was finished and put behind her, and there was another mellow period.

We had a surprise one autumn with the news that the Lutheran Church's Mission Board would like to come for a visit. The Board was headquartered in St. Louis and was responsible for a significant portion of our funding, but in the eight years that we had been in operation there had been few direct contacts. They sent money but had never visited. We arranged a Saturday presentation to include slides, a walk through the neighborhood, home visits with some of our people, a question-and-answer session, and coffee and doughnuts. The whole staff was to be present and participate. We arrived early to put on the coffee and prepare to greet our guests, who were arriving from great distances. Most had come to the city the night before to be on hand first thing in the morning.

Our guests arrived—mostly clergymen—and we were scheduled to begin with a brief introduction and a short morning devotion. In walked Gloria. Since I was working in the kitchen at the moment, Gloria came to me to ask me who all those people were. I explained that the Mission Board had come to visit us, to see where we were located and to get a firsthand feel for our work. She asked if she could stay, and I told her that she was welcome.

Jan introduced everybody, and began with a description of the program and schedule for the morning. When Jan finished speaking, Gloria raised her hand and asked if she could say something.

All eyes turned to her as she walked to the front of the room. Nervous Gloria. Opinionated Gloria. One-of-us Gloria. "I just want you to know," she began, "that I don't know where I'd be without these people. I don't know what would have become of me without the help of The Ministry. They got me some extra money to live on, and when I was sick Tom took me to the hospital, or I would have died in my room. And when my building caught fire, I had no place to come but here. I don't really have family or anybody who cares about me but these people, and I couldn't make it without them, and I just wanted to tell you."

Glorious Gloria. And we call ourselves servants of the poor. It's true—we do our best. But when we become family together, we stop keeping score because it's sometimes hard to tell who's in ministry to whom.

Violet

The newspapers in Chicago had been full of the John Wayne Gacy murder case. Things would be quiet for a while, and then there'd be new excavations at the house—from crawl space to driveway, from driveway to lawn—and another young boy's body would be discovered, galvanizing the papers once again into a reprise of the ugly story.

When we would see Violet she would bring us news of how this was affecting her household. The first installment was that she had regained contact with family in the suburbs. Violet and Bill had moved many times over the years as buildings had changed hands, and their relatives had lost track of them. When their names appeared in the paper, identifying them as the parents of one of the victims, Violet's sister saw the news and immediately got in touch with Violet. It was a happy contact for her, a warm source of support and encouragement.

Violet also told us that her parish, St. Thomas of Canterbury Catholic Church around the corner, had donated money toward a headstone for her son's grave. Violet had been saving a dollar a week out of her food money. The good thing about that was that it left less money for Bill to drink on, but she had to be careful that the amount was small enough that he didn't notice it.

Eventually the newspapers began to carry reports that the Gacy case would be going to trial. Bill became obsessed with the proceedings and traveled across town to the courthouse daily for the whole process. He was there for all the public aspects of the case—the jury selection and then the trial. The court was on the west side of the city, and that required carfare two ways each day. Bill did not miss a day, and that curtailed his drinking. He ate and drank the trial instead. He spoke of nothing else. It was a long ordeal, and the details were horrible. There was testimony about how the accused would lure the boys into his car, then take them home for his pleasure. He often had them around as guests for days before he finally killed them. There was testimony from boys who had been part of Gacy's entourage but who had either escaped or simply been to the home for a party or as a part of a group and had never been in a one-on-one situation with Gacy. There were photographs that tied him to middle-level political events, even showing him appearing in handshake range of President John Kennedy at a local ward fund-raiser in the early 1960s. The shock over where Gacy had been and with whom, and that someone so dangerous had been so public and so close to those in power, elicited a collective gasp among those who discussed the case. This guy got around all right, and he was a real sleaze. How could it have happened? Where was the catcher in the rye?

Bill not only traveled to the courthouse each day, he returned and discussed the trial. He talked about it all the time; it was the only subject he did talk about. Violet and Bill's older son was slightly retarded. He was in his early twenties and had always lived at home. He did not have a trade or a job, and the continual discussion about the court case began to wear on him. He finally left home and moved in with a friend. These days when Violet came for food, it was food for only two people—Bill and her. She'd shake her head in her quiet way and blink and explain that Billy just couldn't stand all the talk about the trial.

The street was not really a safe place for Billy either. It took him away from his father's trial talk, but he was a mentally slow young man, vulnerable to street violence, just as his younger brother had been a physically slight young man at risk of being overpowered by someone who plotted violence.

Then once again, the family's names were in the papers. Once again, they were the victims of tragedy. Once again, the war hero and his wife surrendered a son to violence: Billy was knifed and killed in a street fight. Once again, Violet began to siphon off a dollar a week from her food money to buy a headstone for her last son.

An article was put in our newsletter giving supporters the opportunity to contribute directly to Violet's project, and people donated enough money for Violet to pay for the second gravestone.

Violet had come a long way, from a young mother buying matching sneakers for little boys to the mother buying matching headstones for murdered sons.

Here came Violet, being hauled down the street by two collie- or husky-type dogs, working as a team. Violet was at a forty-five-degree angle to the ground, it seemed, and would have been safer if the dogs had been harnessed to a sled, but she looked resigned, even adjusted. She may have even been contented, but I wasn't. John Gacy had been locked up—the justice system worked. There were headstones for her sons—her parish and The Ministry had supported her, which meant that the Christian community worked. She was in contact with long-lost family because of the news coverage of her sons' deaths—and that was good. But it was not enough.

Nathan

Nathan, not Nate, was unusual because he was so normal. He rarely came to The Ministry because he tried very hard to be self-sufficient. When he came for food, he needed food. No nonsense, no jive. Plain and simple, he needed food. Over a period of nine years I may have visited with him eight times, maximum. He was instantly likable, and he was who he said he was. No nonsense and no bravado—a pleasant man, with dignity and bearing.

As an infrequent visitor to us, he might have been difficult to remember just from a name on the food sign-up sheet, except that Nathan stood out because of two unusual requests: barber shears and paints. Uptown was a part of the city to which unskilled workers tended to drift. Many people had hidden specialties, but that was the exception, not the rule. Nathan said that he had learned barbering in prison so he would have a trade when he got out. When he got out, it was the mid-1960s, and unfortunately people were wearing their hair long. He couldn't find work.

He also learned to paint in prison. He never said why he had been in, and I didn't ask. That was an indication of his demeanor. Many people would have mentioned a reason or invented an excuse. Most people I would have asked. Nathan was not most people.

Along with these special requests was an offer: find him some barber shears and he'd spend a day cutting hair for our people. The request got filed somewhere in my head with the mental note: If anyone ever donates barber shears, they are to be saved for Nathan—if he comes back, that is, because we'll never see him just around. He doesn't hang out. Should we just buy barber shears, even though food is so tight? It was one of those mid-level, ofmoderate-importance questions. It didn't require an answer. It lingered in my mind, occasionally resurfaced, and would again recede. It didn't get erased, however, because Nathan didn't erase.

Nathan had not been around for more than a year, so it was a treat when he stopped in one autumn afternoon for a cup of coffee. He hadn't come for food, just to say that he was doing okay, waiting for some answers regarding job interviews, and by the way, he had purchased some barber tools. Would we like him to come someday to cut hair? It was a delightful offer. Haircuts are a luxury item for the very poor, and this was a wonderful opportunity to offer haircuts to our people.

My anxiety went into gear. Suppose Nathan forgot? Suppose nobody came? Should we post a sign or just nab people who were around on the appointed day and hope that people would be around? What do you think? Should I make a sign? How about you—what do you think? How soon should the sign go up? Should we make a list? Suppose he doesn't come?

The consensus was yes, put up the sign—and pray. I believed in this man and so much wanted him to be who he said he was.

Food days were Mondays and Wednesdays, and super-crowded. We chose Thursday. We opened at 9:00 A.M., so we set the time for the barber at 9:30. The signs were red and white, like a barber pole. On the food days that week we alerted people to the visit of the barber on Thursday.

Thursday came, and the building was empty at 9:00, 9:05, 9:10, 9:15. Suppose nobody shows up? Won't Nathan be crushed? After all these years and all this effort? We'll drag people in off the street. Think. There are thousands of people out there, and we know lots of them. It'll be all right. Oh God, please let him show up—let the people show up. Nathan needs to give this gift and be affirmed for this gift. 9:17. Here comes one. It was Michael Halliday, waiting for the barber, and just a little sugar in the coffee, thank you, no milk. Answer the phone. Run upstairs and write a message. Answer the phone. The twins aren't coming to preschool today, so tell Richard not to pick them up. Run down the back stairs to find Richard.

"Hi. Where do you want me?"

"Nathan—it's great to see you! Come in here to this room where Michael is waiting for you." Thank you, Lord.

Nathan got out his stuff. Shears, comb, soft fuzzy brush, big blue-and-white-striped bib-thing, clippers, talc. I gave him coffee, and he was in business.

The work of the day took over and imposed itself on my consciousness, and I became preoccupied. On a trip downstairs I'd look in and see a new person in the chair, with Nathan chatting away in soft, baritone accompaniment. My day was up and down the stairs, while Nathan's day was in and out of the side living room. There was a steady stream of customers. I stood by the archway, between rooms, and watched, with enough confusion around to be unnoticed. Nathan was different—he was in a role. He was a barber giving the kind of barber service that my husband loves. Soft, relaxing voice, gentle massage to the scalp, yessir, I did see that game. Is that short enough, sir? I'll just brush your neck, and perhaps a bit of talc . . .

An aspect of Christian servanthood is that skill to so precisely care for the needs of a person that the person is able to become whole. The miraculous event of the day was to see whole people sitting in Nathan's chair—people who had been in and out for years, people whom we knew and worked with face to face. Nathan, in the form of a servant, was filling a physical need, and the poor people in the barber's chair were looking whole. They were being shorn on top, but injected with dignity that made them glow from within. It was amazing. It choked me as I watched the transformation in the people and the difference in Nathan. He wasn't shuffling his feet and saying, "Aw, shucks," but he had grown into the awesome posture of the willing servant. He was Christlike. He glowed, and the people were radiant. I slipped away again for a while.

The next time I peeked into the room, Bill was sitting there. Poor Bill, walking around with World War II scars in his head. The disease of alcoholism had been the chaser. Two sons murdered and here he sat, and Nathan was talking to Bill as if he were normal. For that period of thirty minutes, as Nathan talked and stroked and brushed and touched him, Bill was normal, and I was allowed to see that. I turned from that picture blinking away tears.

Nathan wrapped it up at 3:30. A woman who stopped in for

some clothing saw him and dashed home to get her kids the minute school was out. The final customers of the day were two blond cherubs with tickled grins, all trimmed and brushed—obviously the first professional haircuts that they had ever had. On that cloudy late October day, Nathan was my main man.

Julie

$\mathcal{I}$t was a hectic food morning in mid-November of a typical Chicago autumn. There was plenty of bite in the air, and it was a very gray day—gray sky, gray cement, faded trees with hardly a brown leaf left, no sun to brighten the typical yellow brick of so many city buildings, and the threat of snow in a couple of weeks. Smitty called it double ugly.

The building was warm, and it grew to feel very hot on these food mornings with people waiting, staff scurrying, and the press of time: Get the files, don't make people wait longer than necessary, listen carefully, be a good steward of the food that has been donated, be alert to the unspoken other needs, and be a humble servant. Concentrate. Pay attention. Answer staff questions. Think back—remember the details as staff ask for things: Isn't there another bag of small jars of coffee somewhere? I've got someone who was in a fire and needs bedding—Didn't someone from the suburbs recently bring in sheets and stuff? Gloria is a diabetic, so is it okay with you if I give her some of the fancy items instead of the standard things?

There was a file in my hand, and I was bending over Smitty's desk to ask him some questions about the data on the fact-sheet in someone's chart when Martha walked in.

"Smitty! Lynn! I can't believe what I just heard," she began, and we were all ears. "The man in my office who came for food was just talking to me about people, and he said something about Julie and how she used to come here and about how she was hit by a car and . . ."

"What?" we sputtered simultaneously. The babble that followed drew in everyone who was working upstairs at that moment. Staff from the other offices came in, and we pounced on Martha for details and verification and dates. The new agenda for the day was to find out about Julie.

One of my areas of responsibility was to oversee the food operation. If things were too busy to update a person's folder at the close of the interview, I would do it after everyone had been seen or over lunch or even in the afternoon. I always read each staff entry for the day before giving the charts to Liz to be filed. All that would have to wait today—I was going to see Wallace, and Martha had agreed to accompany me.

We still did not believe the information. Certainly with the years of contact with Julie, with all the people we knew, if such a thing had happened, we would have heard instantly.

We took the elevator to the third floor of Wallace's building. The elevators in these old buildings made me retch because they smelled of urine, tobacco, cheap wine, and mildew. It was a toss-up between using them and exposing ourselves to the questionable security of the stairway.

Wallace received us politely. He was sober and subdued, and his hair, pallor, and clothing matched the gray day. He verified the information without fanfare. Julie had been hit by a car late one night and killed. He could not remember the date, but it had been a few weeks before.

Martha and I were stunned—not just to learn the truth, not just from trying to absorb the shock, but truly amazed that no word of this had reached us.

Back at the office, there was a note on my desk from Smitty that said he had talked with someone at the Chicago Police Department. He left a phone number and the date of death, October 13. They would send a copy of the accident report to us.

"October thirteenth? That was a whole month ago!" I yelled, picking up the paper and carrying it back to Smitty's office. Martha came in, Reverend Jim came in, along with Ann, Nancy, and Sister Mary Kay. Richard came upstairs, and our group was a jumble that changed shape as people would leave to answer the door or the phone or when someone came for counseling—and so went the afternoon in a noisy, gloomy haze.

I pulled Julie's chart and went to call her caseworker, Diane. No, she had not heard about it, and she was shocked. For Diane it would mean work. She would have to contact the adoptive family, who would have to inform the children. The court would have to be informed, and the whole complexion of the adoption proceedings would be changed. There was now no case against Julie for termination of parental rights—there was no person with parental rights.

A brief regrouping of staff occurred in the hall, and someone suggested that we should have a memorial service for Julie. That brought some focus to our incredulity.

The memorial service took place after the regular worship service on Sunday. There was a bit of shuffling as some people left, or stretched, or changed seats as the bulletins were passed out for the order of worship for the memorial service.

The service was brief—some lessons, prayers, reflection about Julie by some staff people, and an invitation to others who might like to say a few words. Two hymns were sung. People were subdued—the service was mechanical. People left; no one hung around. There was no family to console, no easily identifiable friend to comfort. People were shocked—I was shocked—but there was not a lot to say. Not this day. I headed home.

I took my seat on the sparsely occupied elevated train and closed my eyes. The tone for the day was reflection. My thoughts wandered to Julie.

I recalled Julie at worship. She had attended services from time to time. Maybe that was one positive thing to say about Julie. In the midst of the chaos that passed for her quality of life, somehow or other Julie knew there was a God who cared for her, a Savior who had gone the distance for her, a Spirit who dared to live, even in her. An involuntary smile came over my face as I recalled a recent note jotted down and left on my desk: "Hi, Lynn. Julie was here for worship yesterday—in her nightgown!"

Ah, Julie, understanding came and went in you—it was there instinctively to know that someone with a baby would need a baby bed (your perpetual quest was the search for one, for others), yet so fleeting, for your own children rarely had a baby bed. No crib for a bed, "The little Lord Jesus laid down his sweet head."

The police report said you were dead on arrival at the hospital. Julie, what were you doing? Where were you going in the rain that night? At 8:50 P.M.? The accident report said 20:50. So precise. "FATAL" was stamped across the report. A witness reported that you were crossing the street in an erratic manner against the light. What was going on? You were eight months pregnant. Many times you had told us you needed to get diapers to have on hand because you were pregnant. Most of the time it wasn't true. We chalked it up to anniversary reaction, as it most clearly synchronized with the time that Jill had been taken. This was no reaction. You had been pregnant. You and your ninth child died together.

It was hard to think of you without children—so much of your life, your concerns, your interests revolved around children. You seemed to want them, to like them, to care about them on the one hand, and to be completely mystified and baffled by and about them on the other—as if someone had run up behind you when your face was turned and deposited several at your feet for you to feed and care for. I always believed that deep down you really wanted to be a good mother, Julie—I did, truly I did, but I just don't think you had a clue of how to do it.

My files burst with letters from Diane, the caseworker, to remind you of your appointments at her office to see the children, and follow-up letters to inform you that you had not been there. Then there were letters to inform you of your right to appear to make an appointment to see the children, and again the letters to notify you that not only had you not followed through on that, but that you were delinquent in your service agreements as stipulated by the court—such being your need to meet with Diane on a regular basis if you intended to get your children back.

There were the phone calls. You would call from my office and scream at Diane, who in good fashion would inform you of your own responsibility to honor the service contracts as set down by the court. You would fly into rages and storm out of the office crying.

A series of strange things happened after Terence and Emily were taken. You wandered out of Uptown and were often staying with people we didn't know. We learned that you'd given birth to twins. The state took them when the nurses discovered that you weren't feeding them—insisting they weren't hungry. Then you'd show up on occasion, often with a child, and report that you were babysitting.

You got married, Julie—for twelve days! You married Stuart as the culmination of an on-again, off-again courtship. It was the only time you ever married. You and Stuart were supposed to counsel with Reverend Jim. Then Stuart sent a note calling it all off, but a week later you and Stuart were married in city hall. For twelve days.

There was a note from Reverend Jim in the file saying that he had been coming home from downtown one evening, late, and had seen you flagging down cars. We were all incredulous. You occasionally would threaten: "I might just as well go back to doing bad things."

"Julie, what are you talking about?" I'd ask, but your face would cloud over, your eyebrows would knit together, your jaw would get a hard set to it, and you'd just repeat, "Oh, bad things I used to do." Did you know what you were talking about? Were you really pulling the wool over my eyes? Or were you just using expressions that you had picked up somewhere?

Julie, it was as if that was the kind of person you were. You borrowed sentences and faces and gestures that you had seen somewhere and put them together to make a person. There is a child's game that has a blank face—Mr. Potato Head—where the child could add a variety of eyes, eyebrows, different mouth shapes and noses, and ears and hair. Really young children would make such funny ones, with an ear on top of the head, or two mouths and one eye. You had the sentences and the faces and gestures, but they were put together in a strange way.

Who were you, really, Julie?

Floyd

The statistics on suicide rise sharply with the onset of the Thanksgiving-through-New-Year's holiday season: loneliness is the worst when people traditionally gather with families. For those who have no families or are estranged from families or have few if any close ties with people, holidays put into sharp focus their singleness. Media bombardments increase a sense of isolation to the ultimate, and despair can flood the emotions.

As Dickens noted, "Want is most keenly felt at this time, when plenty rejoices." Generosity is also most keenly exhibited, however, and the supporters of The Ministry were magnanimous beyond our hopes. The staff always made a list of families to receive Thanksgiving and Christmas baskets, and in the early years the procedure was often frustrating. Half the staff would be out trying to deliver these baskets while the people to whom the baskets were supposed to go had come to the office in need of food, only to be told that someone was trying to deliver some.

In about the fifth year, we changed our procedure. We posted two lists in an office closet, with a fixed number of spaces on each. Each staff person had the opportunity to suggest names for the lists. If a person was on the Thanksgiving list, the name didn't go on the Christmas list, except in rare circumstances, such as having had a fire or being between jobs with no public assistance.

When the lists were compiled, a letter was mailed to the person or family to tell them a date and time for the celebration and distribution of the food. In this way people in need could still come on regular pantry days for food, but we could do something special in addition.

There were many advantages to this procedure. First, we avoided many problems: We saved an enormous amount of time by not having to run around the neighborhood; we did away with the problem of missing people who were not home; and people did not have to stay put to avoid missing their deliveries. Recipients were saved from duplicating provisions—buying a turkey, for example, and then receiving another—and people also were relieved of the anxiety of wondering if there would be anything special for the holiday meal.

The most serendipitous benefit, however, was the celebration. All recipients came at the same time. We prepared a little talk, explained about our supporters and what had been donated, talked a bit about how and why we had chosen them at this time, and often did some holiday singing, had some treats and fellowship, and shared a sense of special community.

The setup was a madhouse. Staff people with short fuses hated it. It was chaotic, and people could be grabby. It was fast-paced, frenzied, and noisy. I loved it. The first task was to list the types of packages that needed to be prepared—the kind of bag for a single, a couple, a small family, a large family, for recipients with special problems, such as a person with diabetes or a family with an infant. Armed with that list, the next trip was out to the garage, the storage place for the food pantry. It was shopping without money, and it was fun.

It also meant a day spent with Richard, sometimes with Richard and Smitty together and perhaps another volunteer who happened by. There were standard items to include—vegetables, canned fruit, and juice. Yet, here were boxes of stuffing mix! How many did we have? Could each person get some? And here, look at this, baby food, and over here, some dietetic jelly and sugar-free cocoa! There's cranberry on the bottom shelf, canned yams in the next aisle, and would you believe it, special English crackers! Scoop and gather, fill the bags, tell jokes with the guys, tease and be silly, almost like a day off while we were working like mad dogs at the same time.

Several times we'd be interrupted by phone calls or by other staff who needed things from the pantry or by suburban friends delivering food collections from supporting churches and church schools. There was a lot of lifting and carrying, and an overwhelming surge of thankfulness toward the supporters who were always prodigal in their giving. There was only good for me in this part of the process—pure pleasure.

On the day of the celebration, we'd bring the thirty or so bags into the building and group them by numbers—all singles under the kitchen table, doubles in Jim's office, small families on the back porch, large boxes for big families in the back hall. Names were marked on the bags with markers so they could be easily identified as we often added the special treats for people according to taste: dietetic candy for Gloria, the diabetic; canned pudding for Oreste; baby food for Ingrid; and black olives for Emil.

As the time for people's arrival approached, the pace picked up. Smitty had gone to the bank for a stack of two-dollar bills, and he and Reverend Jim were busy stuffing these into envelopes. That tiny bit of green money would give each person the dignity of some choice, even though small, about what was added to the meal. Some people were cleaning the downstairs living room and dining room and arranging chairs for the gathering; some were putting on more coffee and setting out trays of cookies, crackers, and cheese; and the rest of us were running up and down the stairs adding the "fresh items." Often bags of apples and oranges had been brought in, and these were added to the bags—Let's see, what do you think? Three oranges and three apples for the singles? What about the couples? A bag for families? Are there enough? Here, I'll give you two of these, give me another apple, and Duke has no teeth, so make his oranges only. There's a boxful of homemade frozen applesauce, so let's add a bag to each, okay? Good. Look at this, small jars of coffee! Who do you think should get these? We've only got six jars.... Get the phone.... There's another delivery in the driveway.... Richard's gone out to pick up Reba, so take my key and ask them if they need help to unload....

The people began to arrive this pre-Thanksgiving afternoon, and the hum picked up, and we all went into overdrive. There was a lot of laughter, staff bumping into one another on the back stairs, a feeling of going "up the down staircase" and overwhelming goodwill.

Into this atmosphere came Floyd and Virginia Hansen. I had met her only once, when I picked Floyd up the day we buried his dog. Virginia had never been over here before. I gave Floyd a nod as I scurried up the front stairs to grab something from an office, and was startled to have Virginia intercept me as I hurried down the back stairs.

I hadn't really talked to her that I remembered and was struck by her small build and her deep Gravel-Gertie voice. It was a funny voice on that small woman. She was going on and on about material, saying, "It's all prewashed, so nothing will fade or shrink. Woolite is good for washing, and everything is well stitched. We really appreciate this." I decided that the woman was half mad and that was why she'd never been over here with Floyd. I smiled, said, "um-m, nice, uh-huh," a couple of times, then slowed down but without breaking my stride, slipped bars of soap into the bags that were around the kitchen.

Virginia dogged my trail, however, and I couldn't get away from her. As I was carrying the rest of the soap to the bags in other places Virginia pursued me and kept talking, "It was so nice, but I'd like to see where it is if you don't mind. . . . Out in the yard under a tree, that's what Floyd told me." I suddenly realized what the woman was talking about.

"Oh, certainly, Virginia, of course, yes, it is under a tree. Come with me," and I took her by the hand to show her where their dog had been buried. I had been off in never-never land! "Here's the spot, Virginia, and you're welcome to hang around out here a bit if you'd like, but would you excuse me? I really need to get back." She was fine about that—I should just go about my business.

Reverend Jim was speaking, telling people how we valued them as people and celebrated their lives and the relationships that we had with them, and how, because of the generosity of The Ministry's supporters, we could give this added treat. Several of us said a few words, then we sang a bit, and as the distribution began, we brought out the munchies.

I was hustling into the kitchen for a bag for someone when once again I encountered Virginia at my hip. "It's okay if you use Ivory, that will work. I made one for that other woman but never heard a thing about it. . . ." What was it with this woman? "Uh–huh," I said, reaching the living room and smiling as I handed the bag to one of our single gentlemen. ". . . And it's in a big box, but your name is on it. . . ." She was like gum on a shoe. I turned to face her.

"In there," she pointed, "that's where Richard said to put it, so Floyd did." And then she left me alone.

Someone called for another bag, and I was running again and forgot about Virginia. People were leaving and Jim was passing out the envelopes with money, and we were assisting some to the van for rides home and helping people out with bags. It was eventually quiet, with the soft buzz of fading conversation and laughter going out the door beyond the front porch, when my eyes fell on this big square box under the kitchen table, and I remembered Virginia's words. I slid the box toward me, and sure enough, my name was on the side. It was taped shut, so I reached into the drawer for a kitchen knife, slid it sideways under the tape, and opened the flaps. There inside the box was a homemade quilt! It had large, irregular pieces, crazy-quilt style, of bright, primary colors with a variety of fabrics. My mouth just hung open. Woolite. Ivory. Washing instructions! Virginia had been giving me directions about how to wash the quilt!

I pulled the whole thing out of the box to examine it. There were dots and solids and fabrics reembroidered with yellow flowers. There were wool, polyester, double knits, cotton, and blends. It was reversible. What an offering! What a labor of love! Here I'd thought the woman to be half mad and had hardly paid any attention to what she was trying to tell me.

I sat on the elevated train, lucky to have a seat, and cradled this enormous square box. It was sitting on my lap, high enough that my head just rested on top. I was so giddy that I was giggling in my mind and afraid I would burst out laughing any minute. I felt in possession of such a wonderful secret, but I didn't know what the secret was, exactly. Part of it was that I had this wonderful quilt, this quilt of many colors. Like Joseph, I had been singled out for a special gift.

Emil

*I*n 1980 in Illinois, a single person on public aid would receive a general assistance check for one hundred and eighty-nine dollars, plus fifty-two dollars' worth of food stamps and a green card. Food stamps were good for food only. My good old German grandmother used to say that it did not cost anything to be clean. She was obviously never on welfare. Food stamps did not buy soap, toothpaste, deodorant, shampoo, laundry detergent, a comb, toilet paper, shaving cream, razor blades, or sanitary products.

Food stamps would not buy OTCs (over-the-counter medications), either. For example, a person could not buy a dollar bottle of generic aspirin or a three-dollar bottle of cough medicine or antacid tablets, but could go to a doctor who would write a prescription, and the expense of the doctor's visit and the prescription drug would be covered.

The bill would be paid, that is, if a person had a green card. The green card authorized medical-care payment from the Illinois Department of Public Aid. In addition to being the ticket for payment of medical care, it was used for identification at most agencies such as ours. It contained the person's name, current address, and birth date; if the green card was for a family, there were also the names and birth dates of all those who would be covered.

In 1980 in Uptown, the average rental for a basic living unit for a single person was about one hundred sixty-five dollars. What that got you was a living room with a Murphy bed in the wall, closet, or cabinet, or a hide-a-bed sofa, plus a bathroom and small kitchen. The kitchen had a sink, sometimes a regular stove with an oven, and a refrigerator. There might be a combination stove top with a small refrigerator below, where one would expect to find the oven.

The single person, then, who paid one hundred and sixty-five dollars rent had twenty-four dollars in cash left over. Fifty-two dollars in food stamps for a month meant roughly twelve dollars a week for groceries. The extra cash would be used for transportation, paper products, and any simple medications. It was tight, but possible.

The first cut in general assistance checks brought them down to one hundred and fifty-four dollars. There was an outcry of public outrage at that terrible occurrence, and no sooner did people get oriented to it than the check was slashed again, this time to one hundred forty-three dollars and fifty cents. People who had scraped together enough to pay their rents the month before were now really in big trouble.

The ways people coped could cost dearly. Some would sell their food stamps. They would use a dollar food stamp to purchase a very small item, such as a can of corn—then pocket the change and continue to buy one item at a time with each dollar food stamp, accumulating the silver until there was enough to pay the rent. This was a rather sophisticated approach, burdensome for the individual as well as the store clerk.

Things finally crashed to a halt when the checks were cut to one hundred thirty-nine dollars. Impossible is impossible, and no one knew what to do. Landlords fared no better: They could evict people for nonpayment and have no tenants and receive no rents, or they could continue to allow tenants to be in arrears and at least receive something. It was a bad situation.

A young and idealistic go-getter from the state's attorney's office called one afternoon to brainstorm about who could possibly testify in court about the problems that were caused by these cuts. The young man, Matthew, came to the office in mid-afternoon and explained what he had in mind.

A class action suit was being prepared against the state of Illinois. The judge who was hearing the case was an Irish Catholic, as was the young attorney, but the judge had stated publicly that the only people who were on general assistance were lazy young men who should get a job. The task was to determine whether the stereotype was true, and if not, to find people on general assistance who did not meet this stereotype and who would be willing to testify.

We used a notebook for the sign-up sheets for food days. Each page was dated and numbered, and the folks who came for food would sign their names. It was simple to go through the book and collect data such as how many came on which date, which day; how many were singles, families, couples; and how many people we served in a day, week, month, year, and so on. I got the book from the rack above the slot where we put the food charts that were pulled on food days and scanned the names. Eliminate the families. Eliminate the illegals. Eliminate the couples. Eliminate those on Social Security or SSI. Eliminate those who were not articulate, who did not speak English, and those who were disoriented or drifty and who could not be relied on to appear in court.

I wrote down possibilities as I came to them, and the number was really very small. Out of that small number, choose any who have been employed until recently. Put a question mark by those who have not been around for a while, who may have moved or got work. Three names were left.

I took the list, looked up the names in the files, wrote down the current addresses, and followed Matthew out to his car. It was the perfect car for an idealistic young man—an old VW bug, probably as old as he was.

We tried the first name and address and had no luck. We drove south six blocks and west about three. The next address was at the edge of our area. The building had a spartan look about it. It was yellow brick, very plain, and had a locked entryway. It was a key-only building—no buzzers, no bells—and it looked like another strikeout until someone happened to come out. We smiled, held the door, and slipped inside. We could not find a staircase, but there was an elevator that we rode to the third floor. I hated to do this to the poor man who lived here. I was not 100 percent sure that he would even recognize me. He had been to The Ministry and to the food pantry for several years, but he came very rarely, maybe once or twice a year—although in the last six months it had been six times.

We knocked on the door and Emil opened it. I introduced Matthew, explained briefly what Matthew was looking for, and Emil invited us in. The apartment was very spare, very plain, very tidy. It resembled Emil—vanilla. Fair of countenance and balding was a more accurate description, but more pale than anything. The apartment had no frills, no color, no smell, no nothing. Emil had on an olive color shirt, a pair of gray wash pants, and slippers. He was a heavyset man with a round, doughy face that resembled line drawings of Alfred Hitchcock, except that Emil's face was rounder and he did not have a protruding lower jaw.

Emil listened quietly to Matthew as he explained the problems. Emil was well aware of the hardship the cuts were causing him. He agreed to help, "if I can," he said. The case was being heard the following Wednesday at one o'clock at a courtroom downtown. I promised to pick up Emil at eleven-thirty that day. He said he would remember. I wondered.

Matthew left me at the corner of Montrose and I hopped the elevated train home. I had been so absorbed in this dash around the city for a person to testify—kind of caught up in the melo-drama of it—that I had not paid attention to the time, and it was after six-thirty when I got home. My husband was upset with me because he had been worried.

The court date arrived, and it was Ash Wednesday. As good as his word, Emil was ready and waiting for me. We took the el down-town and located the building, then rode the elevator to the elev-enth floor. The elevators opened onto a long corridor that intersected with another hall and more elevators. The opposite wall of that corridor was all glass and provided a striking view of the city. The corridors were packed with people who had come to tes-tify and to hear the case. A few of them I recognized from the street, some were familiar faces from the Public Welfare Coalition, and there were workers whom I had seen at area food pantry meet-ings and those who had gathered to give testimony at the Chicago City Council some years before. We were truly an odd collection of dissimilar people gathered to testify about one specific problem: the impossibility of surviving on one hundred and thirty-nine dol-lars a month.

Matthew lined up all the people who were scheduled to testify, and we went in to take seats. The remaining ranks filled the chairs and benches in this ultramodern courtroom. The interior of the room was brick, and the side of the room opposite the judge's bench was shaped in an arc. There was carpet on the floor, oak-stained medium-brown benches and woodwork, and offset light-ing. The large wrought-iron clock visible on the brick surface above the judge's bench showed one o'clock, and people began to watch the doorway and scurry for seats instead of milling around. They continued speaking, but in hushed tones.

The judge entered, and the process began. The first to testify was a nun. She was sworn in, and as she took her seat facing the attorney and the spectators, the ashes on her forehead stood out in sharp contrast to the white that framed her short navy-blue wimple. She operated a food pantry in a local church, and spoke movingly of the hardship imposed on her people by the cuts in aid. Two other nuns spoke, repeating a similar story, each with unique embellish-ments and details that tugged at my imagination and made me gasp. I watched the judge. His face was like a stone.

A landlord spoke. This was no slumlord. He had a large building consisting mostly of single-person units. All his tenants were in the same dilemma. He was not about to throw them out—they had no place to go and he would not have any tenants to replace them, but what was he supposed to do? How would he continue to supply heat? electricity? water? How would he pay the taxes? Again I watched the judge. His face remained stony.

I was sworn in. I answered the questions about how many people came for food, what was the percentage of increase since the cuts, how many were singles as opposed to families—an inter-esting item, because many food pantries did not serve singles; singles were expected to ferret out on-site meal programs—Who funded us? How much? What was the volume of food? and so on and so forth. I could not see the judge behind me. My stomach was full of stones.

One of the food-pantry workers had brought a middle-aged woman who was sworn in and spoke of her plight. Poor thing—fifty years old and alone, unmarried, unemployed, the picture of a lonely, forgotten person, brave in a henna rinse and blue coat. The judge was leaning forward. His hair appeared to grow whiter be-fore my eyes, but the impression was caused by the rush of blood that reddened cheeks. His brows were knit together across his stony face.

Emil's name was called, and he stood up and walked forward to be sworn in. The bailiff walked over to Emil and asked him to place his hand on the Bible and to raise his right hand to be sworn. When Emil turned to the man he was in perfect profile to where I was sitting. He looked very plain. He wore khaki pants, a simple, light-colored plaid cotton shirt, and black shoes. His head was mostly shiny bald with a tonsure of thinning gray hair. His very round, brown eyes were a little rounder; his cheeks were a little fuller and corresponded harmoniously with his round belly. As he raised his right hand, I could see that Emil was shaking so hard that his hand moved back and forth across several stripes in the plaid as he was being sworn. He took his seat.

"Name, please."

"Emil."

"Are you employed?"

"No, sir."

"When were you last employed?"

"Two years ago."

"How long were you in that job?"

"Twenty-two years, sir."

"How long have you worked, sir?"

"I left school at sixteen so I could get a job and help out. I worked for the post office and delivery services. I've worked all my life, but there just isn't any work to be had that I can do. The company I worked for closed down. The labor agency that I worked out of has no work. My blood pressure is high now, and there's certain kinds of work I can't do anymore. I'm not supposed to lift things."

"How old are you, sir?"

"Fifty-six."

I watched the judge. His eyebrows were raised. There was some expression on his face now, but I could not read it.

A few more people were sworn, then a local alderman and some state representatives. The state rested. The defense rested. The judge retired to chambers, and there was some brief milling around. When the judge returned, we all snapped to attention. The testimony had been great. There were no two ways about it—the case had been heard, yet we did not expect anything. This judge had a reputation for harshness.

Maybe the ashes got to him. Maybe it was the meek, lonely spinster or the quiet, unemployed Emil. Maybe it was the holy day that pricked this Catholic judge's conscience. Maybe, just maybe, it was simple justice.

"In the case of the People of Illinois against the State of Illinois, my judgment is for the people. Case dismissed!"

There was silence while the verdict sank in, then some cheers and some handshaking all around. Matthew and I praised Emil, who flushed and smiled shyly, and congratulations were heard all around. A holy day indeed. Even in the Chicago Circuit Court, it was a holy day.

I smiled and smiled. I tried not to think about the reality, which was that, verdict or no verdict, if the legislature did not appropriate the money, it mattered not one whit what the judge said.

Richard

$\mathcal{R}$ichard Walker was deaf in one ear. I could never remember which one, but if I were talking to the wrong side, he would lean his head down, tilt it to one side, put a finger behind the good ear, and state that he hadn't heard, and to please begin again.

Richard, a young widower, came for food sporadically and regularly, meaning that when he was working we didn't see him, but if he was out of work, he needed food. In the nine years that I knew Richard, he never collected welfare. He was a burly guy with a friendly face, blue eyes, thick, wavy, sandy-brown hair, clean shaven, and neatly dressed.

Richard worked out of what was called the "slave market." The term referred to the day-labor organizations that operated out of Uptown—most of them located on a strip of Broadway Avenue, between Montrose and Leland, 4400 north and 1100 west. The day-labor places had contracts from suburban companies—factories, warehouses, almost anything—for workers. The contracts could be to supply a worker for a long-running job, a seasonal job, a week's job, or day work, and the company paid the labor organization an hourly rate per person. The labor organization, in turn, hired workers from the street, supplied bus service to and from the destination, paid the worker the minimum wage, and pocketed the difference. To get a "ticket" was a first-come, first-served situation. The day-labor offices opened at 5:30 A.M., which meant getting up at four-thirty to get to the place before it opened and get a prime spot in the line, enhancing the chance of getting sent out on a job.

If there was work and if a person got a ticket, the bus left early for a job that might begin at seven thirty or eight and might take up to two hours to reach. After the shift was over, the worker returned and was given a check for minimum wages for the number of hours worked, minus a charge for bus fare. A really good worker who was requested specifically by the foreman at the company could get on a regular ticket, which meant that some of the less-dignified procedures would be circumvented and the person had a more or less steady job for the duration of the work. A person could also be a "no return" (not called for a second day) but could try for a ticket for another company or go to a different day-labor agency. Over the years, those who worked regularly out of the slave market had worked them all and were known by the kind of work they did.

When a person arrived back in Uptown after the day's shift, the person might have been occupied for fifteen waking hours and needed to find a place to cash a check. Often the currency exchanges were closed, and the only place to cash a check was the local bar, which charged a two-dollar fee, beer or no beer. The pittance that was left made this practice a very exploitive one. Richard was a regular in the slave market and often got a good ticket, so if there was work anywhere, Richard was one of the guys sent out.

If we didn't see Richard for food, it was quite probable we would see him for worship. He had grown up in a Lutheran orphanage. Since a majority of our people in the early years were Appalachian white or black, the religious backgrounds tended to be Baptist, Methodist, or some fundamentalist church. Of the people we served, Richard was the only cradle Lutheran who came through our doors. He was at home and comfortable with Lutheran liturgy and the Lutheran hymnal. We used it rarely, more often substituting a large-print edition of familiar hymns, but when we did use it, Richard didn't miss a word.

Richard's personal history was sad. He was put in the orphanage in early childhood, sometime before school. He was thought to be retarded because of his poor hearing, which was the result of an abusive home situation before he was institutionalized. As a young man, he married a woman named Carol, and they had two sons, Dennis and Frederick. Carol developed cancer when Frederick, the younger son, was about two. Richard described Carol's illness and death graphically. When she was dying and frightened, he had promised her that he wouldn't leave her. The realities of the hospital, the arrogance of the medical personnel, and the procedures did not deter him from keeping his promise. He was told to "remain outside," but he would have none of it, sitting by her side and holding her hand through the grim ordeal, the examinations, and the painful death.

The financial realities of life were grim for a single man whose extended family lived states away and who needed full-time child care for preschoolers. Richard lost his modest home and sent Dennis, who got to be unruly as he became school age, to live in Minnesota with his maternal grandparents. Richard gravitated to low-income housing, and when steady jobs ran out, turned to the day-labor agencies.

When we first met Richard and he chronicled this sad tale, he would say, "I don't cry so much anymore." He was quite aware of his feelings and matter of fact, though graphic, in his description of events. He was a veteran, and he said he used to draw. I was always glad to see him when he showed up.

Frederick was a sweet child and a comfort to Richard until he developed a form of his mother's disease: large tumors would spring up in different parts of his body, be treated, recede for a while, and then attack a new site. Richard was exhausted with stress and worry.

One day one of our parishioners came in to tell us that Richard's son Frederick had died. He didn't know any of the details, had heard the news "on the street," and that's all he could say. I got on the phone and called all the local funeral parlors and everyone else I could think of to see if there was any record of a funeral for a six-year-old boy. Everything came up blank. The parishioner had also said that following the funeral Richard allegedly had taken the body to Minnesota for burial. In the afternoon Martha and I went calling. We went to Richard's building to see if his landlady knew anything. Not only did she know nothing, beyond a report similar to the one we had heard, but Richard's rent was due, so she hadn't locked his apartment—it was available.

Martha and I went in. It was quite a mess, but certainly not the worst we had ever seen. It looked as though someone had grabbed a few things and left in a hurry. The landlady was obviously going to shovel out whatever was left and then rent it, so we went around collecting things we thought Richard might want: all personal things such as photographs, cards, and letters, a few books, and odd bits of good clothing—all of which fit into one brown paper bag.

Several weeks later word filtered in to us that Richard had been seen on the street—he was back in town. We passed the word that if anyone ran into him, please ask him to come by, we'd like to see him.

Within a week, Richard came in and went upstairs to see Reverend Jim. They were closeted for a long time. The lights under the phone buttons showed that a lot of phone calls were being made, some rather lengthy. The phone use is easy to notice on a day when several staff people have a list of calls to make. Make sure no one's on hold, update charts, and check the phone again.

The story we finally heard was that Richard had simply come to the end of his rope. He was unable to care for Frederick. The prospect of a sick child who might die, the endless search for neighborhood people competent to care for Frederick and whom Richard could trust and afford, had grown so overwhelming that Richard was no longer able to face the stress. He packed a few things for himself and a few for Frederick and went downtown to the bus terminal. He explained some of this to Frederick, then left the boy on the bench, knowing that he would be found, taken into protective custody, and well cared for. Then Richard disappeared for a while.

Jim checked with the Illinois Department of Children and Family Services, put Richard in contact with the caseworker for Frederick, and made plans for Richard to meet the caseworker. Meanwhile, Richard explained the details of having left Frederick, plus Frederick's health situation, who his doctor was, what medication he needed, and so forth. Jim was able to intervene on Richard's behalf so he was not prosecuted for having abandoned Frederick.

A routine of visits was established so Richard could maintain contact with and support for Frederick, and a closer connection was made with Dennis, who was now in his teens. Richard came to use our phone and speak with his in-laws, and on two or three occasions Dennis came to visit.

Richard looked a bit less haggard, but at about the same time work really slowed a lot and was bad enough that several day-labor agencies were opened only for half days or would close for days or weeks at a time. Richard was around more and needed more food during those times, yet he still resisted the prospect of applying for general assistance. He did not see himself as that needy a person, and at our Christmas open house, where folks came for music, lots of treats, fellowship, and a gift for all, Richard assured us that he really didn't need anything.

There are many memories that come to mind when I think of Richard, but the strongest is a picture. It was a lovely Sunday in July, and I was the worship leader that day. It was a sunny day and the turnout was good, the fellowship was warm. In the middle of a hymn I happened to look up and really see Richard. He was standing in the front row, wearing a neat brown suit, a clean brown shirt, a yellow tie, and a lapel cross. His hair was slicked down, and he was singing so heartily and wearing such an earnest expression that I was momentarily transfixed, then had to avert my glance. It was the Transfiguration, and it made my vision blur.

Sammy

*A*bout two years after Sammy first came in for food, he began to hang around. He'd drop in on nonfood days to chat, have a cup of coffee, or just visit with other folks who were having a cup of coffee. It was a safe place. It was off the streets. It was out of the elements, and Chicago had lots of "elements." Mainly, it was a warm and inviting place, and all staff people were genuinely glad to see familiar folks and foster this casual fellowship. We also fanned the flame of the more intense fellowship of worship, and Sammy even showed up at church from time to time.

He was a funny guy. In his early seventies, tall, gray, and of medium build, he had a hop, skip, and shuffle walk. He was hard to understand, as toothless old people are, but his Southern black dialect was thick and made Sammy doubly hard to translate. I was a New Yorker by birth and could understand a Brooklyn cabby, but had problems with a thick Southern accent. I was improving with on-the-job training, though.

Once when Sammy was there for food and I was interviewing him, he was in a fit about his tomatoes. He had cultivated a little portion of a vacant lot near his building and planted some tomatoes. He could see them from the window of his high-rise apartment and had watched in anger as neighborhood toughs picked the just-ripened delights. They did not take them to eat, but threw them on the ground, dashed them against the fence, splattered them on the sidewalk, and pelted one another with them.

Sam was disgusted—he retaliated by firing his gun.

"You did what?" I gasped.

"Oh, I didn't shoot at 'em—just over their heads. Scare 'em off. It made me sick!"

I kept shaking my head. "Sam, you have a gun? You keep a loaded gun in your apartment?"

He was blasé and reassuring. "It's not a totin' gun, ma'am!"

Sammy had a friend named Clemmie he liked to hang out with. If Sammy was hanging with Clemmie, chances were that they were both half lit, but they were never obnoxious, rude, or sloppy—just red-eyed and a little more difficult to understand. In an area with a high population of alcoholics, Sammy probably was not one—he just liked to tipple some.

Sammy was married, and had been, to the same woman for almost fifty years. Her name was Thelma. She was very heavy, very religious, very tidy, and she had a serious heart condition. She came with Sam on one or two celebratory occasions and wore neat patterned dresses with stockings and jewelry and looked a bit "upscale" compared to Sam, who wore jeans, a herringbone jacket with suede elbow patches, and a tweed golfing cap over his salt-and-pepper hair.

One day as I was headed upstairs to my desk, I noticed in passing that he and Reverend Jim were having a little howdy-do smile session in a doorway, with a hint of furtiveness about it. Sammy pressed something in Reverend Jim's hands. Jim came into the room and walked into the closet, chuckling. The safe was in there, and he explained that Sammy had come by to give him some money. I raised an eyebrow and looked up, waiting for the story, while Jim fiddled with the combination. He said that Sam had come in once to give him three dollars, and Jim said he'd put it in the collection, but Sammy had insisted that it was for Jim. Rather than argue with him, Jim thanked him, accepted it, then put it in the safe. This had been going on for over a year. The amounts varied, but it was two or three dollars a month. Jim had been putting it in the safe in our petty cash envelope.

In February of 1980, Jim suffered a stroke and was no longer able to work. He tried to visit, but his visits were sporadic and very difficult for him. The money-passing routines continued, with Sammy giving me the money now, and I was the one putting it in the safe. This continued, and I gave it little thought beyond thinking that it was "sweet."

In August of that year my father was diagnosed with cancer. When I was worship leader on Sunday soon after that news, as I was asking people for the names of those we should pray for, I explained about my father and added his name to our prayers for the sick for the day.

Later that week Sam came in and asked for me. I met him at the back stairs and he stood there, cap brim in his hands, and said, "Heah's some money for Reverend Jim, and heah's a dollah fo' yoah fathuh."

That stopped me cold, and I protested a bit, saying, "Wouldn't you like me to put it in the offering, Sam?"

But he was adamant. "No, ma'am! It's fo' yoah fathuh!"

Now Sammy did come for food now and again, but he drew Social Security and was, in Uptown, in the most unusual position of also receiving a pension. He received a twenty-three-dollar-a-month pension from the Jays Potato Chip Company. He lived in a pleasant apartment in an attractive new senior citizens' high-rise building on Sheridan Road. Though he would still be called a poor man by the standards of American society, his life was more stable and happier than most, and all his basic needs were met.

I took the money upstairs, put "Jim's money" in the safe, then sat down with this dollar. The poor man's dollar. What to do? I flapped it like a fan, thinking. Of course, I'd put it in the safe. My father was very comfortably well off—it seemed like stealing to send him a dollar from Sam. Yet, that was Sam's choice. Just because I was a staff person, did I have the right to overrule his wish? Who was I to say that my decision was better than Sam's? Most important, it finally seemed, was that I had no right to do other than what he wished with his money. It was, after all, Sammy's money, and if he decided that my father should have it, so be it.

I took out some Ministry stationery and wrote to my father: Dear Dad . . . I explained who Sammy was, how he had heard about my father, and that he had given me the money. I wrote of my dilemma and said I was passing on the problem to him. I suggested that he should do something special with the poor man's dollar—have an ice-cream cone on Sam, something, but consider that it was from Sam.

My father called. "I got your letter. I don't know what I'm going to do yet. I'll let you know."

What he did was buy stamps—at that time you could buy six for under a dollar. He copied my letter and wrote a cover letter. These two letters he mailed to his church and a few other organizations in his town. He solicited donations on behalf of The Ministry and made a generous donation himself. The poor man's dollar was a seed—not only seed money for soliciting donations, but also a seed for understanding the disproportionate generosity of the poor.

Harold and Rita

$\mathcal{H}$arold, physically, was *The Wizard of Oz*'s Scarecrow come to life. He was lean and lank, had stringy gray hair, small dark eyes, a beak nose, and a rashy red face. He was slightly stoop-shouldered, which made his arms appear to hang in front, hiked his coat jacket up in back, and gave him the appearance of the scarecrow on a pole. He had the watery-eyed, rheumy appearance of a drinker. He was simple—a nice enough sort—and he came for food once a month.

Hal spoke of his wife, Rita, who had a bad heart, giving that as the reason for his coming by himself all the time. We had never seen her, although people in their building confirmed that Hal had a wife. He also spoke of a son, Jerome, who was nineteen and lived in a residential placement in a distant suburb. The return of Jerome became an elusive and reappearing thread that wove in and out of our dialogues for years.

One fine summer day Martha and I decided to pool our lists and make our home visits together. We stopped at the closet for goodies to take to the various people we would visit. "Look, over here— someone donated a box of costume jewelry. Let's take a necklace to Hal's wife, don't you think?"

We knew we wanted to visit Hal and Rita, so we had chosen another family who lived in that building, plus two more families on that block and a family in a building that we'd pass on the way. It was a nice day, and we strolled along with our treasures, relaxed without the noise and push of a food morning, warmed by each other's company and the summer day, and feeling gratitude toward the many who so generously donated food, money, and the myriad treats to the people of The Ministry community. Everything seemed to fit. We made a few stops, visited with people a bit, and made notes of additional needs they had.

When we knocked on the door at Hal's, he was decidedly surprised to see us. He squeezed his body into the narrowly opened door to block our view of the room. After he made a few over-the-shoulder remarks, we were ushered in. The apartment was small and tidy, and the yellowed shade was drawn on the sunny day, giving a look of a 1930s sepia-toned photograph. Rita was a pleasant-looking woman with a dumpling face, an apron, and one blind eye, and trying not to look with the other eye at the bottle of Jim Beam that occupied the place of prominence on top of the refrigerator. Years of home visiting had made us skillful at the quick glance— good both at how much we could take in and at what we noticed that others were trying to hide. So that's the scoop—they both drank!

When, later, there was a fire in their building, which was two blocks south of us, they moved a block north. Hal continued to come for food, continued to talk about Rita's poor health, and continued to talk about how things would be when his son came home. Jerome had been gone for sixteen years, and at this point it was apparent that Hal and Rita would never be able to care for the boy—he must have been removed from the home and taken into protective custody, rather than being voluntarily placed.

The building to which they moved housed many of our people, and as such, was a hotbed of gossip. One of our people came in one day to tell us that Rita had died. The word on the street, as we checked this out, was that not only had Rita died, but apparently she had been dead for some time before Harold realized it. One of our staff people met Harold on the street, and sure enough, Rita had died. He came over to talk to Reverend Jim about it and to plan the funeral.

On the day of the funeral, Reverend Jim went to the funeral parlor and was met there by Rita's brother. He was a pleasant man, an average person who lived in a more middle-class part of the city. That Harold had been able to maintain contact with him was amazing. Many of our people lost contact with family members. Very few of the people we served had a phone. If they were a little slow, like Harold, and couldn't remember a relative's number or address and couldn't contact the relative, it wouldn't take long before all contact was broken. If a person has a fire, as in the case of

Rita and Harold, or a building is condemned, or the rent is raised and people move, how do relatives find them? If a person does not have a phone, a job, or a driver's license, it's almost impossible to find the person.

One other staff person, Milt, was at the funeral parlor with me. No Harold! We surmised that he had forgotten—a very probable explanation. Milt left to track down Hal and returned with him in about fifteen minutes. Milt had spotted Hal standing on a street corner, chatting with some neighborhood folks. Milt reminded Hal about the funeral, and he hopped right into the car and came into the funeral parlor sheepishly. He walked over to the casket, was startled, and began to cry, "Oh, Mommy, oh, Mommy, no. . . ." Hal and Rita had been married for more than thirty years. Whatever semblance of normalcy Hal maintained, this sustaining relationship could be considered the pattern as well as the product.

Hal chatted a bit with his brother-in-law, who was quite gentle with Hal and helped him through the service, which, brief though it was, was still an ordeal.

Rita's death not only affected Hal emotionally and socially but also meant a change in income. Paying the rent for his apartment and paying for groceries without benefit of his wife's disability check was very hard indeed. We encouraged Hal to apply for disability, and he did—over and over and over. He kept getting denied. I would look at Hal and wonder how he could be denied disability. He was semiliterate; he was of minimal intelligence; he was unskilled, a nutritional disaster, an active alcoholic in his late fifties, and couldn't even remember to attend his wife's funeral! Who could he work for? What kind of work could he do if he even remembered to show up? Could he work for us at The Ministry?

Finally we persuaded Hal to reapply. We helped him with the paperwork and were very adamant about his bringing all mail for us to see, so we wouldn't miss the court date. Hal was good—he remembered, and he complied. We decided that an early-riser staff person would get Hal and put him on the elevated train. I would meet the train at the Chicago line and escort him to the courtroom in Evanston, where he would be interviewed by a judge who was hearing this appeal.

I got to the station, got off the train, and waited for Hal. Good deal—we found each other and boarded the northbound shuttle train for a bank building in Evanston. We walked in, searched the directory, and found the judge's chambers where we were supposed to be. It was probably the first case of the morning because we didn't wait, just walked right in. The judge was very personable, introduced himself, shook hands with Hal, asked me who I was and what my relationship was to Hal. I explained who I was and handed the judge my business card, and he agreed that it was fine for me to stay. The hearing began and the judge asked all sorts of reasonable questions, and Hal gave all the appropriate answers—appropriate, that is, if I had given them, but they sure were not appropriate coming from Hal.

"Harold, would you like to work?"

"Yessir."

"Harold, can you take care of yourself all right?"

"Oh, yessir."

"Can you fix your own meals?"

"Yessir!"

This continued for a bit, the judge routinely shaking his head and cooing, and I could imagine the personal sketch he was composing. It consisted of about eight check marks, and the bottom line would be *SSI denied.* I asked the judge if I could ask Hal a few questions to clarify some things, and he was very agreeable.

"Hal, can you tell the judge how you got here this morning? Who got you at your apartment and put you on the train?"

"Smitty," he said. Most of us called Milt "Smitty."

"Who paid for the train, Hal?"

"Smitty."

"Do you remember when your wife died—that you forgot the day of the funeral."

"Uh-huh" (*cries*).

"Who found you and brought you to the funeral parlor, Hal?"

"Smitty."

"The judge asked you if you can take care of yourself okay and feed yourself. Where do you get some of your food, Hal?"

"From you and Reverend Jim and Martha at The Ministry."

"Did you have a dog, Hal?"

"Yup."

"What happened to him?"

"He died" (*sigh, giggle*).

"Didn't your neighbors give you food to feed the dog, Hal? Bones, I think?"

"Uh-hm-m."

"Who ate the bones for the dog, Hal?"

"Me."

The judge looked sick. He was wide-eyed once or twice, carefully followed the dialogue with his eyes, and when we were finished he smiled, said thanks, it had been helpful, and shook hands with us. We left. It felt good. If SSI were denied this time, at least we would all know that someone had heard Hal, and if someone thought he was a good candidate for a job, so be it. At least we would not have to wonder whether the right questions had been asked.

Hal's SSI was not denied. He did receive it. That meant he would receive more money than the very small amount of general assistance. Of course, once Hal received SSI, he drank more. It was a Catch-22 situation. Was it right to go to court so Hal could receive more money, which he would then use for alcohol that would kill him quicker? If he didn't receive SSI, would it have been right to deny him food at the food pantry? If he weren't denied food at the food pantry, would it have been right to give him food and turn someone else away? Especially if he were eligible for SSI and the other person had no other resources? There's no happy ending. There are only wrong answers. That day the good guys may have won one in court, but they lost the battle on the street.

Reba

It was a pleasant afternoon in August, one of those days when you first notice that the days have begun to gather darkness to the outer edges of their daylight hours, and I was appreciating the warmth as I walked the two blocks west to Winthrop to pay a call on Reba.

Reba lived on the first floor of a green stucco house. There were red geraniums on the stoop on either side of the door, and I could see Reba walking onto the enclosed porch shortly after the ring of the doorbell.

She was her gracious self and invited me in warmly. Visiting Reba felt like cheating. Everyone on the staff loved Reba, so it did not feel like work to visit her, and because of this there had been times when she could have been overlooked. Reba was always in church on Sunday and usually came to the office on Mondays to cook a noon "dinner" for the staff. She loved visits, though, and it was a time away from the bustle of people and phone calls to check in with her.

Everyone called her Rebie. Once I asked, "Reba, how do you spell your name?" and she said "R-E-B-A—Rebie." Okay. Reba was from the South and had lived in Uptown nearly twenty years. She had never married or had any children but had lived with her sister. They did everything together, were devoted to each other. When Reba's sister died, the people at The Ministry became her anchor, and her nephew and his family were her tie to her sister.

Reba had been on my mind because Ann, our deaconess, had told me on Monday that something was wrong with her. Ann had seen Reba in church on Sunday, and Reba had told Ann that she was having pain in her mouth and having difficulty eating. As soon as Reba opened the door, I understood. The left side of her jaw was swollen—she looked like a squirrel.

Reba was bustling around and had been baking—not at all unusual for her. If she wasn't pickling beets, making apple butter, or baking pies, she was sewing. Today she had been baking and offered me some apple pie, which I accepted eagerly. I perched in her kitchen taking in the atmosphere as she gathered plates and forks and napkins and cups and began to pour the coffee that had been waiting ready on her stove.

The kitchen was a 1930s kitchen. There were large cabinets with doors made of thin tongue-and-groove boards, a metal table with white porcelain-enameled top and an oilcloth tablecloth, white painted wooden chairs, all carefully placed by a window overlooking an honest-to-goodness backyard with grass and real raspberry bushes, smack dab in the middle of the city! There were large-patterned print curtains, large canisters for staples, a single white porcelain sink with ridged drainboard side, canning jars filled with preserves and pickled beets, and a single overhead light. The kitchen was tidy and comforting. It was a grandmother kitchen. A wave of contentment washed over me as I sat there munching the pie, drinking Reba's coffee, absorbing the atmosphere of another generation, and listening to Reba, in her soft drawl with her quaint expressions, describing what she had been preparing that week.

Following our midafternoon feast Reba took me into her room to show me her projects. She had been busy sewing little favors and treasures to take to people in the nursing homes. It was a project that Nancy had been working on with several women in the Bible class, but Reba was having a fit. Nancy was on vacation, and the other women refused to do a thing until she returned. I smiled as we walked into the living room to sit for a while. I did have an agenda, something besides eating up all Reba's goodies, but it seemed important for her to air a bit of what was on her mind. I knew she did not do a lot of venting, though she was not a pushover or anybody's dummy, either. (Once Reverend Tom asked Reba to take in a girl who was coming off heroin cold turkey. And Reba did!)

She was on a roll right now. She had made some tiny bonnets for children. I had never seen bonnets exactly like that—at least, not up close—and was fascinated. They were the kind of bonnet that women used to wear in the cotton fields in the South, she told me, and that was the jumping-off place for Reba's speech.

"I don't believe all these people who say they're from the South are, or else they'd can! And they'd take care of their home. People want folks at The Ministry to give 'em everything same's everyone else gets, yet they won't work!'"

She sounded like a political conservative, and it made me smile. Reba had the right to say it, though, because she had paid her dues.

I looked at Reba and let my eyes roam around the room. It was a woodsy-looking space—the windows had glass curtains and, with the attached glazed porch, the daylight was diffused, making dappled splotches around the room. There was a couch with an afghan over the back, a small bookcase with books, a coffee table with a Bible on it, three armchairs, each with an antimacassar on the back and covers on the arms, a floor lamp by one chair and table lamps by the others, a rather ornate and attractive end table with marquetry, doilies on the tables with occasional incongruous plastic flowers next to potted plants, and some cute bric-a-brac.

When the phone rang and Reba went to answer it, I strolled over to the buffet behind the table in the dining area and looked at the photographs. There were many, and I'd seen them before, but when Reba returned to the room she walked over and told me who everyone was.

Reba was in her early seventies, a big woman, about five feet nine inches tall and quite hefty. She had straight, narrow calves and small ankles, wore brown oxford shoes, gaily colored blouses, and dark A-line skirts—except on Sunday, when she often wore a pink dress and matching pink straw hat in summer, and a dress and coat and hat in winter. Reba never wore slacks—and I doubt seriously that she owned any. She had horn-rimmed glasses, her dark, steel-gray hair was close to her head under a hair net. Her complexion was what would be called olive, I suppose, but she was a Negro. She would never have called herself black, and it would not have been true anyway. The photographs explained it. There were blacks and whites and mixtures, many generations' worth in the photos, and somehow it was hard to believe that Reba gave it much notice one way or the other, except to note that they were "her family."

She was much too dignified to have been a statistic in anybody's cause, an individual who would not be bound by the limits of any race's claim as its own. If anything, she defined herself as a Christian woman and, beyond that, as "Southern." So when she scoffed at those who didn't can, yet claimed to be from the South, I kept quiet.

We sat down together in her living room and adjusted ourselves, each preparing for our face-to-face, "What is this visit really all about anyway?" revelation. I told Reba that Ann had mentioned talking with Reba in church on Sunday, and that Reba hadn't been feeling good. Reba told me that she did have a call in to her doctor and would keep us informed about what was happening. She seemed fairly calm, but her face was very swollen and alarming to look at, and in spite of her apparent serenity, she confessed to some anxiety. I made a mental note to check in with Reba regardless of whether I heard from her, thanked her for the pie, gave her a hug, and returned to the office to attend to the rest of the day's work.

Reba called me the next morning to say that she had a doctor's appointment for the next week. The doctor did not know about the tumor, and she was not in any pain. The call receded into the background as the events of the day picked up speed: Jimmy, a preschool child and friend and neighbor of Martha, had two more tumors; there were calls from IDCFS regarding the return to the mother of a failure-to-thrive baby; one of our street people, a recovering alcoholic, came in to practice on Ann's guitar. In the afternoon there were thank-you letters to write, including one sad one that I kept recycling to the bottom of the pile. It was to a family who had sent us fifty dollars in memory of a son who had died.

Two days later Reba called, but this time she was in pain. I went over immediately and drove her to the doctor's office. She would be there for a while, so I returned to the office and instructed her to call when she was ready. This time there was progress: She was going to be admitted to the hospital in the morning.

Dear Reba, I thought, blessed with innate wisdom and a woman in whom grace is personified, be well. Reba was calm, but there was now a quiet that had settled over her—a different kind of quiet. It was an expectant hush, a frightened intake of breath, a very fragile quiet.

The next day was Friday, my day off, and Milt Smith (Smitty) took Reba to the hospital. I checked with him in the afternoon to get Reba's room number and see how things had gone in the morning.

When I called Saturday night, Reba was sounding very low. She told me that the doctor had told her that her jaw was decayed. She had two days of X-rays, and the doctor had been in to see her just before supper. He said, "We have a real problem. I don't know what to do." I told her to sit tight—I would call Milt and we would be back in touch with her.

When I reached Milt on the phone, he was ready to storm the hospital. He suggested I check with some people about procedures for transferring patients to other doctors and hospitals, and meanwhile he would talk with Reba.

A little later he called me to compare notes and give me some marching orders. To Reba he said, "Reba, be ready at ten thirty tomorrow morning. I'm moving you to a better hospital." To me he said, "I will pick you up in the morning at the Lawrence Avenue train station at ten."

The only proper response was, "Yes, sir."

I awoke in the morning to that first snap of cold that comes as a shock in early September after an August heat wave in Chicago. It was a cool and misty morning, and I dressed in lady clothes to help me feel authoritative. What I really felt was a bit nervous and more as if I were playing Tonto to Milt's Lone Ranger. I was on time, important in doing anything with Milt, and of course he was early, which always made me feel late and him a bit impatient.

It was a small city hospital, one square lump on the corner of a nondescript, narrow street in a pleasant neighborhood. There were apartment buildings all around, and it looked as if it had been a hotel at one time. Once inside, one could see how tiny it really was. It was immaculate. Reba said that the food was excellent and everyone was wonderful; it simply was not equipped to deal with complicated medical problems.

We entered the lobby prepared for trouble and rehearsing speeches about who we were, what we were doing there before visiting hours, and why we should be let in. The lobby was empty. No one was at the information desk. The place was deserted, so we looked around and headed for the elevator. So far so good. We got to the third floor, Milt took a chair, and I glided quietly down the hall to Reba's room to see if she needed assistance dressing. She was almost ready when I arrived, and while she was tending to the final items of shoes and hair, a nurse arrived. She was dismayed by the sight, yet when I said that we had come to take Reba out, the nurse was helpful and said she thought she had better call the doctor.

I left Reba to gather her things while I went to tell Milt. We walked up to the nurses' station and introduced ourselves, and in no time she had the doctor on the phone. Milt told the doctor the plan, and the doctor was relieved. He agreed that it was a good idea to take Reba someplace else, that he really didn't know what to do for her, and the hospital was not equipped to do the testing that would be required to find out what she needed.

We whisked Reba out of there, hardly able to believe how easy it had been, and Reba breathed a sigh of relief. Milt also called her nephew, and he planned to meet us at Ravenswood Hospital. The admission process took a while because Reba did not have a doctor at that hospital, so someone had to be assigned to her. By early afternoon, however, things were set, Reba was settled and more relaxed, and we left her to visit with her nephew.

Reba called on Wednesday. Things were not good. After three days of tests the plan was now to have a biopsy. Reba was very low. "You know, Lynn, September and October have always been hard months for me. I had a brother who was shot at that time, and my mother and sister both had birthdays in those months and both died in those months. When it comes nigh to September, it feels like a bag is over my head. When October passes, it feels like I've just taken off a tight shoe."

Reba had the biopsy, revealing malignancy. But when the tumor was removed from Reba's jaw, to the doctor's surprise, it was benign! The staff was elated. It was the talk of the day. Everyone was amazed and overjoyed at what was truly a miraculous event.

At dawn on the fifth day Reba went into shock and was rushed to the Cardiac Intensive Care Unit. On the eighth day she was returned to her regular room, and on the fifteenth day she went home.

At the office we all said that Reba would not have been alive if she had stayed at that little hospital. We knew it—we all knew it. Reba said it differently, however. Reba said, "Smitty saved my life." She was right.

Oreste

When the odor from the filth in Oreste's apartment seeped out enough for the custodian to call it to the attention of the management, new living arrangements had to be made once again for Oreste. He had escaped from the Somerset because he wanted more pudding, and it took two months before we found out where he had moved.

This time on Kenmore, one block west and two blocks north of our building, seemed like the ticket. The facility was a well-established concern, and the atmosphere was pleasant. There were varied levels of care, depending on a person's need, and it would be able to accommodate Oreste both as he was and as he might be if his health declined, which we deemed likely as a result of normal aging and the inevitabilities of poor hygiene, variable nutrition, and a heart condition.

Oreste knew the drill by this time. My battles with establishing my right to arrange this for him, to lock him up, as he put it, were battles that ranged on familiar territory, and once again Oreste moved. But he did not go gently. He complained, crabbed, carried on, and threatened for months. Then one day the social worker at the Convalescent Home on Kenmore called. Oreste was gone. No one saw him for weeks. He was clever, and he must have bought groceries at midnight because in his escape escapades he really went to ground, with nary a clue to his whereabouts.

Eventually he was comfortable enough to come out of hiding, and smug with his independence, he presented himself to us again. He often needed a little something—two cans of tomato soup and some spaghetti, his favorite food. On one of our walks together, he showed me where he was living—in a roomette arrangement in a three-flight walk-up, directly across from the Convalescent Center!

Cute, Oreste. And we were worried that maybe you'd been run over by a bus!

Oreste ate his breakfast out every single morning at the tiny diner set at an angle on the corner of the block. Not only did he eat there, he ate well there. Every morning he had coffee, juice, eggs, sausage, toast, and hash browns. It was not very realistic. He was running a tab, and it was costing him fifty dollars a month, almost the total allotment of food stamps per month for a single person. Wonderful. Oreste would not listen to any talk about how this was not working, and when the day of reckoning came, Oreste could not see the problem.

Unhappily, the situation was resolved when Oreste got sick and wound up in the hospital. All I knew was that I had not seen him for a couple of weeks—not too strange in and of itself, with so many hundreds of people in and out of the office all the time. With no reason for alarm, it was a simple case of "out of sight, out of mind." My summer vacation fell at this time, also, so by the time I returned I had not seen Oreste for more than a month. There was a note waiting on the desk for me: Oreste was in the hospital. That Thursday, with Jackie Raino along, I stopped at the hospital to see him.

"Oh, Lee, Lee!" Oreste yelled, and began to cry a bit. The nurse in the hall hurried in, startled at his response. We were the first visitors he had had, and he had been there for five weeks.

His appearance shocked me. There are cultures—certain Native American cultures, for example—in which when the elders deem it time to die, they climb into bed and die. Oreste had lost a considerable amount of weight. He had never been heavy or thin, but looked average, filling out clothes in a totally unremarkable way. Before, while his swarthy complexion might be scraggly with beard stubble, his cheeks were smooth and his forehead over his heavily arched brows was also smooth. Not anymore. His face was deeply lined, his cheekbones protruded around the hollows of his face, his brow line jutted out at a sharp angle, and his gray eyes were deeply sunken. He was clean, wearing a blue-and-white hospital johnny, and he was hooked up to a heart monitor and two IVs—one with saline and one with glucose. Following the excitement of first seeing us, he settled down and got quiet, his deep-set eyes following every move either of us made.

I sat next to him while Jackie walked around on the other side, standing. She chatted away and held his hand, then the other hand, and asked him questions about how he felt and whether he had any pain, saying "Oh, look at the color of your johnny," and "What's this machine?" and so on. Jackie the volunteer was being friendly, but Jackie the RN was checking his pulse, looking for bedsores, observing the color of his fingertips, and giving him a professional once-over.

There was the obligatory television suspended from the ceiling about eight feet beyond his head, and now the noise broke through to our awareness. "Do you watch TV, Oreste?" Jackie asked.

His eyes closed, his eyebrows elevated ever so slightly, and he turned his head just a slight bit to one side and said, "Why, sure," in the tone of voice a person might use with someone who had asked a very stupid question with an obvious answer.

"Who got married yesterday?" continued Jackie, not put off by Oreste's condescension.

His eyes opened and he gave her a sidelong glance from his still-angled pose. "The king of Wales," he said.

Well, he passed the reality orientation test, for it was true. Prince Charles of England, the Prince of Wales, had married Lady Diana Spencer the day before; it was all covered on television, and Oreste knew what was going on. Maybe he would be okay.

The hospital discharged him, but it was apparent that he could not care for himself, so he was once again admitted to the Convalescent Home. When I stopped in to visit him a few weeks later, he was not doing well at all. He was hitting people, a very unlike-Oreste thing to do. Oreste did not exactly have friends, but neither did he have any enemies, with the possible exception of Arthur, a young and painfully thin man who hung out at The Ministry all the time and whose birthday we had been celebrating the day Floyd's dog was buried. Oreste was always teasing Arthur, and Arthur, in whom patience was not manifested, ever, would fly into wild rages and storm around. Oreste just shrugged. Extremely frustrated with this apparent baiting, I asked Oreste why on earth he bothered

Arthur. He could see that Arthur hated to be teased, so why persist in doing it?

"Ah," Oreste shrugged. "I can see he's unhappy, so I try to make him laugh." A method in his madness. How could a person quarrel with that?

The following month was filled with Reba's hospitalization, so I did not see Oreste for about five weeks but included him in the next visiting day. Floyd and Virginia were first, and I took them some cut flowers from my garden; then on to see Reba, just recently out of the hospital; Sarah; and finally the next two blocks north to the Convalescent Center to see Oreste.

Like a cat with nine lives, Oreste continued. He would reach the brink, look like a candidate to have "words said over him," as Smitty would say, and then he would bounce back, admittedly more frail each time and now visibly aged. When I found he was not in his room, I was afraid he had died, but today, amazingly, the man was downstairs in the living room playing bingo!

Fire

The evening news was dramatic and ghastly: There had been a huge fire at the Royal Beach Hotel—a transient hotel in the northern part of Uptown. Once an elegant tourist site, as were many buildings in the area, it had fallen on hard times and been washed in the tide of the city's poor as they emigrated north, the latest victims of the gentrification projects that forced them out of their previous neighborhoods.

"Hey, come here, Mom. Do you know where this building is?" the kids called to me as I was preparing dinner. I went in to watch the newscast. The Royal Beach was on the far edge of the area that was served by The Ministry, and while a majority of those we saw were families who lived in apartments, there were still single people who lived in hotel rooms and managed by heating their food on a hot plate, or, in more desperate circumstances, by warming a can of soup on a radiator.

The newscaster was calling this the worst fire since the great Chicago fire, and as the dead were carried out and counted the newscaster was proven accurate. Nineteen people had died and fourteen people had been injured as a result of the Royal Beach fire.

We scanned the papers at work the next day, and to our surprise found a handful of names of people we had known. One man had been in for food earlier that same week. None of the people were well known to us, but we knew them just the same.

The newspapers and radio and television broadcasts were seeking assistance from the community in identifying several victims who remained unidentified. As the days went by, then a week, then several more days, Martha and I began to fear there could be more people we knew. We chose an afternoon when we could clear our calendars and headed downtown to the morgue.

Martha had done this before because she and Richard had managed an apartment building for some years. The two of them were about as unshockable as they come. It was a first for me. The ride downtown on the elevated train was rather subdued. Martha and I had become good friends over the years, visited back and forth with our families, and chatted on the phone, but there did not seem to be much to talk about today.

The building was a long brick building, and inside there was a stillness about it that was like being in another world. It was not the vibrant stillness of a cathedral in midday or the windswept stillness of a cemetery or the stillness of a home when "not a creature was stirring, not even a mouse." It was an airless stillness. It was a stale stillness. The smell and sensation of formaldehyde sought my nose and oozed back into my memory. There were no groups of people around in conversation. There were no plants. There must have been offices or rooms, but I did not see them. All that stretched out before us was corridor linking corridor linking corridor.

Someone on duty directed us to an elevator, and we took that downstairs. A man met us at a door and ushered us into his office. He was looking for three names—the others had been identified—and he opened a drawer, withdrew some photographs, and slid them across his desk gently. It was hard to imagine how anyone would be able to identify these people. The photographs were so "other" that they almost were not shocking, yet it was totally shocking that the pictures were so strange.

The people in the photographs looked like melted toys. They were only partially there. It was numbing. We shook our heads sadly, handed the photographs back to the man, and left.

Conversation about the fire sprinkled the talk in the mornings as food people sat in the living room drinking coffee; it came and went in staff meetings, the staff prayer and Bible study group, and talk on the street, and it was used as an example in our outreach conversations and presentations to supporting churches in the area. The building had had no sprinkler system, no smoke alarms, no warning devices whatsoever.

In the course of conversation, one of our staff quoted a staff person from the Catholic Worker House around the corner, who said that in the deaths of poor people it was usually the staff who were the mourners. The quote danced in my consciousness. It was a familiar experience. We did a lot of mourning for our people—when they drank, did drugs, were robbed, beaten, raped—and when they died. So many people seemed to have no one, no family—no parents, siblings, relatives. We had conducted funerals for people where, for the most part, we were the only mourners, save a neighbor or two and maybe one in-law.

Not only were so many people alone, but they were also nameless on the street. Even those who were recognized by friends or hung around with people often did not use names. Maybe they used a nickname or just a first name, but there was this great sense of namelessness.

> "Thus says the LORD . . . :
> 'I have called you by name, you are mine.'" (Isa. 43:1)

The words of the prophet Isaiah kept coming into my head, and a picture of a banner at church flashed in front of my eyes. That's it! The Ministry was the keeper of the names. We were the ones who knew so many of these people. We needed a banner. We owed it to our people. We knew them. We remembered them. We knew their names.

It was to be a simple banner—white cloth, sturdy and closely woven. The top said, "For all the saints . . ." and the bottom said, "Alleluia." For several weeks we went back in our memories and files and listed the names of all those who had died—all the people who had been part of The Ministry since the beginning. We called former staff people and read the list to see if any had been forgotten. When no one could add any more names, the names on our list were put on the banner. In black ink were row after row of names, written with indelible marker. The most recent names were the names of those people we knew who had died in the fire.

The banner hung in the hallway by the staircase and was a backdrop for worship on Sundays. It was also one of the first things people saw when they entered the building and what the food people faced as they sat in the living room drinking coffee and waiting to be interviewed.

The banner was finished and hanging in time for All Saints' Day, the first of November. There was a good bit of space left, as the names were small, and more would be added as time went on.

The approach of Thanksgiving and Christmas always meant lots of attention from the media. It was not uncommon at this time of year to walk up the steps on a food morning and find that the first person in line was someone from the network news. The coverage was always very favorable to the organizations that distributed food and sympathetic toward the plight of the poor.

One morning when a crew was in, after the taping and interviewing by the anchorman the cameraman began to ask questions. I showed him around a bit, explained some of our operation and some of the specific problems, and on his way out the door he handed something to our receptionist. She came over and handed me a donation of one hundred dollars in cash—from the cameraman!

On November second, the day after All Saints' Day, there was a call from a reporter for the *Los Angeles Times* Midwest bureau. He asked if he could come to talk about hunger in the city at this particular time. He was charming, and he asked all the right questions: Was I skeptical? How had I gotten involved? What did my family think of this? It was a chance to state everything I believed in. Then he asked if I had always been terribly religious. It made me laugh, and I said, "Terribly, no, but seriously, yes."

The photographs on the wall over my desk were a great source of stories, and I told him several. A feminist friend from church had given me a green button with "59¢" written on it in white. That year, it was reported that, in general, women workers earned fifty-nine cents for every dollar a man earned. No one in the office knew what it meant, but the reporter did. We shook hands warmly, he said he'd send a copy of the article when it appeared in print, and I walked him down the stairs.

At the foot of the stairs he glanced around as he was getting ready to leave. Then his eyes fell on the banner. He cocked his head a bit, and I explained about All Saints' Day and all the people we had known who should have someone remember them—a place where their names were written down—and about the impetus behind it, the fire at the Royal Beach Hotel. His lips tightened a bit, and he focused more carefully on the names for a moment. Then he looked up at me somberly.

"I covered that fire," he said quietly.

The Crying Child

*O*n a long food morning in the days when Oreste was still living independently, a full list of people had come in, been seen, and been served. After I had finished my interviews, I read the entries of the day on the charts of the people I had seen and the notes the other staff people made of their interviews. These comments gave me a good overview of the myriad needs of the population we served.

At lunchtime I wandered down to the kitchen in search of my yogurt and another cup of coffee. It was a lovely summer day, and some of the staff people, ready to take a break, were headed for the backyard to sit under the tree for a few minutes. Each one carried a milk crate from the back porch on the way out, and we sat and visited for about fifteen minutes.

When I went back inside I found Oreste waiting. I gave him some coffee and found a few Three Musketeers bars for his pocket. Then I went upstairs for the Monday staff meeting. There some outreach speaking engagements were assigned, and arrangements were made for those who volunteered to give tours to groups scheduled to visit. We checked and rechecked our coverage for the vacations coming up, dealt with a few problems we were having with some drop-ins, and dispersed in about an hour.

Downstairs, Oreste was still sitting on the couch smoking and drinking coffee. I would not want this man smoking in my home— he smoked very short, nonfiltered cigarettes and often dropped them on the carpet, then stepped on them! I would scream and yell and carry on when I saw him do that, and he would shrug his shoulders, cock his head, lower his eyes, and go, "Eh."

I had some errands to do in the community, so Oreste and I walked up Sheridan Road together, enjoying the pretty day, the summer air, the lightweight clothing. That is, I was enjoying the lightweight clothing; Oreste was wearing a jacket, as always, and a brown fedora.

I walked into the Somerset with him, and with no plans to stay, was about to leave when there was a flash in the distance across the large lobby, followed by shrieks and screams. At the far end of the room were tiers of balconies overlooking the lobby. I saw the elevator door open on the next level, followed by similar shouts of alarm. Trina was on the warpath.

The Uptown area of Chicago had a large number of mental patients who had been released from a psychiatric hospital or ward after being stabilized on medication. They took with them a prescription for continuing medication and the address of a mental-health worker in the local area for follow-up. In our area, the facility for continuing care was the Edgewater-Uptown Mental Health Clinic. The theory was good, but in practice it did not always work. There were always the Trinas who, when their medications ran out, became very unstable, did not have the understanding to refill their prescriptions, and as the days wore on, became more and more disoriented. Many would pace the streets from the break of dawn until nightfall. They were never home for follow-up calls by the mental health worker and therefore fell through the cracks of the system.

Trina was in her fifties, had frizzy gray hair that stood out around her head in an aureole, was always filthy, was always smoking, and was often talking to herself or yelling. Her eyebrows were always knit together in a scowl. She was feisty when she would come into our office for a can of tomato soup. When she came, someone had to be on full guard because her smoking was so dangerous. Trina would drop out of sight every so often and be gone for months, and when she reappeared she would be cleaner, a little heavier, and quiet. Gradually, as she either ran out of or neglected to take her medicine, she would become more and more wild.

On this summer day she was in full swing. Staff people began to run around, and soon people were visible on the balconies of the various floors, popping out of elevators, peering into rooms, and scuttling around trying to find Trina. Then there would be a new scream from somewhere, and the people would move as a wave toward the noise.

I suggested to someone in the social-service office that she call the police. "Oh, we just want her out of here—I don't think we need the police."

"You may not need the police, but Trina does."

"Do you know this person?" the social worker asked me.

"Yes, she's Trina, a sometimes patient at a Chicago mental hospital. If you just shoo her out of here, she'll be on the street, a danger to herself as well as others, because sooner or later someone's going to deck the woman. But if you call the cops, they won't arrest her—she's sick. They'll take her to Reed, where she'll get some attention and some medicine, and be okay—for a while, anyway."

The worker called the police, and they arrived at about the same time that Trina, bashing people left and right, was being herded into the vestibule. We all met face to face in the tiny ten-by-ten space, the cops packed up Trina in the back seat of the blue-and-white, and off they went.

As far as I knew, none of us at The Ministry had ever had a real conversation with Trina, so we did not often think about her until something really strange happened. One day an incident reminded me of Trina and the myriad lost people like Trina—who fall through the cracks and resurface with strange and indecipherable scars. Liz was on vacation, so I was sitting at the reception desk on a food morning. It was the end of the month and I knew it would be busy, but it was even busier than I expected. We had readjusted our policy to include five extra families on the last two food distribution days of each month. The theory was that the single people could always get food at the congregate meal sites, but it was difficult to bundle up a houseful of children and drag them around.

When I got to number twenty-five I could see the line still extending to the door. Some of the people I recognized as single and knew that even though inconvenient they would be able to eat elsewhere. While I was writing the names of family people, a woman came up beside me and said, "Put my name down." I knew her—she was Charlotte, a younger version of Trina, and just as unbalanced. I explained that the list was now full, that we could only take a few extra families. She began to yell and scream and demand that I write her name. When I said no another time, she belted me in the side of the head. I was stunned. This was a first. Other than childhood spankings, I had never been hit—and never in the head! I felt a veil of calm come over me as I continued to take the other names, but I was aware of a flurry of activity. Someone hauled her upstairs to talk with Reverend Larry. I poured coffee for two and took them each a cup, then went back downstairs.

Other staff were around, serving the coffee to those who began to take seats while they waited to be seen for the food interview, getting a count from the list to begin to bag up the groceries, and bringing out the eggs, milk, and bread that we purchased to add to the bags of groceries. I went to the door to give someone directions, and as I closed the door behind me and turned back into the room, I couldn't move. The shock of having been hit finally penetrated, and I was as if paralyzed. I just stood there holding the doorknob with one hand behind me, unable to do anything. Nancy happened to look my way and came running.

"Come upstairs," she said. I was still stuck in that spot, but she undid my hand from the door, put her arm through mine, and walked me step by step up the stairs and into my office, sat me down, and got me a cup of coffee.

As time wore on, the shock of the incident became worse. It was hard even to explain. I was not angry with the woman—she was ill. I was not frightened—I was never really in any danger, and there were people all around who could have protected me had the woman become more violent. I was not worried about an impulse to strike back—it had not even occurred to me. But something was wrong. I could not shake it, and I could not name it.

What happened to people who were really hurt? who were injured? who were raped and violated? What about people who were terrorized and pursued and whose homes were broken into? What must it be like for all those people—people who really were in danger? If I was feeling so strange and was basically safe and unhurt and not even annoyed at Charlotte, what was going on?

The feelings of strangeness persisted for days. When I talked about it to people, I got a sort of blank stare. One evening I was riding home on the elevated train, too tired to read my book or write notes but not tired enough to sleep, and I watched the names of the stops as they appeared at the window. Chicago was so orderly. It was neatly divided going north and west, so each sign would tell what hundred north and what hundred west it was. "LOYOLA" the sign read, and gave its numbers north and west.

Ah, Loyola. My memory drifted back to the clinic, my first volunteer project, the little play group of children who were siblings of psychotic children. During the four years that I worked with that group, I met many of Pat Barger's doctoral students plus the social-work students and trainees, and I met many children, observed many therapeutic situations, had lots of discussions with Pat, and received a wonderful education. I smiled thinking of them—Todd, who first talked in our group; the twins, Steven and Stanley—one pulled hair, the other bit kids; Nelson, with the electric-shock shoes, whom we tried to keep from breaking glass; Phoebe, who my Andrew complained, "always eats all the cookies—mine too!" and Nicole.

Nicole. Comfort-the-crying-child Nicole. Between infancy and early childhood, Nicole had had many operations and had had an inordinate amount of pain for a small child. She had arranged this experience in her mind to figure that any time a child cried it was because some adult had hurt her or him. Therefore, taking Nicole anywhere in public was very risky.

If Nicole was in the grocery store and a child began to cry, Nicole would immediately turn on the accompanying adult, usually the mother, and begin kicking her in the shins. This happened over and over in public situations. It happened at the clinic when other children would cry and Nicole would begin to assault the closest adult.

Her therapist suggested a phrase to help Nicole: "Nicole, comfort the crying child." A great deal of time and work was needed to help her change, but it eventually began to help. When a child would cry, Nicole would look quickly for the nearest adult. When she heard the therapist say, "Nicole, comfort the crying child," her whole body would quiver as she fought for control. Finally she would reach out her hand, quite rigid with the heel of the palm extended, and very gingerly pat the crying child as the therapist would praise her and reinforce her action.

The phrase had been very helpful to me in rearing my own children. "Comfort the crying child." Of course. In school, on the playground, in the neighborhood, if a child gets picked on or hit, what happens first? Often the guilty party gets yelled at, dragged in to the principal, sent home to the mother, or disciplined in some way. And the crying child?

Charlotte, poor Charlotte, had sat upstairs in an office, drinking coffee and receiving a flurry of attention. I was the crying child, mercifully rescued by Nancy, and still waiting for someone to comfort me.

Sarah

The people with whom I had long-term contact had a grip on me that was not always easy for me to understand. It was natural to keep close ties to the ones who were mellow and likable, but some of the others may have hooked me because of guilt or because of something familiar about them—something that may have reminded me of a long-forgotten person. Sarah was like that.

Sarah was old even before I went to work at The Ministry. When people spoke her name it was often accompanied by a heavy sigh and a shake of the head. It was difficult to feel good about much of anything after an encounter with Sarah because she was never satisfied, and she was very demanding and self-deprecating and she whined—all at the same time.

She was more than eighty years old when I first met her. She lived around the block in a high-rise senior citizens' residential hotel. She had what would be called an efficiency apartment—living room with a studio couch for sitting by day and sleeping by night, a bathroom, and a pullman-style kitchen. It was cramped, but it was relatively decent—certainly a cut above the tenement buildings around. There was a main desk, a security system, some minor activities available in the building during the week, an intercom system, elevators that worked, and maid service that included fresh linen weekly.

Sarah would come to The Ministry for "just a little something." She would shrug her shoulders, close her eyes, raise her eyebrows, and say, "I don't ask much—whaddaya givin' out today?" Whatever it was would not be good enough, of course, but Sarah would let us know in no uncertain terms that whatever it was, it was the least that we could do.

In the early days, food had been distributed more casually, and sometimes people went to the basement of the storefront building to be served. It was in just such a situation that Sarah had come. Her eyes were not very good—in her words, "My eyes, ah, what can I say?" and she'd shrug and turn palms out toward us, looking helpless. Sarah fell down the back stairs, a concrete set of steps that turned at a ninety-degree angle. Sarah, poor eyesight, eighty-plus years old, her little stooped body a showcase for her internal misery, had broken her arm. She was picture-perfect for a case of staff guilt.

"Sure, give her a loaf of bread. After all, she broke her arm. Good grief, of all people to have that happen to, it had to be Sarah! Yeah, I know, I know, but just remind her, it's only once a month, and tell her that next time she has to sign up."

She would not, of course. It was part of the game. To receive food, people had to sign a list, and they could get food one or two times a month. Sarah refused. After all, all she wanted was "a few little things." It became a power struggle between the two of us. Other staff people let it go—they either gave food or didn't—but with me it became an issue. It seemed necessary that she "understand."

Eventually her eyesight was too poor for her to go out of her building unescorted. Since she was then on a local Meals on Wheels program, she really did need only just a few things. Sarah became a regular for my home visit list. Before setting off, I would pack a small parcel with "a few little things." Ah, Sarah will be pleased.

"O Lynn-dear, I'm so glad you came. It's terrible to be so alone—just like a little dog. I don't know how I ever ended up like this. What's in the bag?" and she'd follow me over to the table and start to empty the bag. Bread. Soup. Tuna. Fruit. "No Jell-O? Gave it all away to the others, I suppose. Oh, well," she would sigh, pushing the other things aside, and I would lose my resolve not to bite. The next time I would remember. Jell-O! No matter what, don't forget the Jell-O! And I wouldn't. But it didn't matter. Something else would be missing. "No pudding? Well, nobody's perfect. I guess you can't go back and get me some pudding?" Rummage, rummage. "I could really use some coffee. Got any cookies in here? All I ask is a few little things. . . ."

I would jump to the bait, explain that we usually did not deliver things this way, it was just a little gift for her, and she would quickly begin to whine and complain about her eyes, how tragic it was that she had been a widow for so long, a disgrace that she had never had children, was so all alone, worse than a little dog, and how lucky I was to have such wonderful curly hair, and I'd cave in, exhausted. Back at the office I'd stamp my feet and go into a tirade about how I was not going to visit that woman anymore—she drove me crazy. It was impossible to satisfy her, and she didn't need anything anyway. The other staff people smiled blandly and ignored me.

Sarah had come from a very large family of Russian Jewish immigrants. There had been about a dozen children in the family, who had arrived here when she was very young. Over the years Sarah forgot exactly how old she was, but she had been one of the older children, and only two besides Sarah still survived. She had lived on the West Side with her husband and worked in a clothing establishment. A photograph of her on her wall—a youngish Sarah, with a sharper face but basically recognizable as our Sarah—showed her wearing a marvelous, broad-brimmed hat with a bird at the band on one side, all set at a daring, rakish angle. She was barren— a great shame to her as a Jewish woman, and a great sorrow to her in her loneliness. Her husband's death in his forties had devastated her. She was still grieving, forty years later.

My strong resolve not to see Sarah and get hooked by my own frustration never lasted very long. I noted in the file that her birthday was the second of February and decided to bake her a small birthday cake. It was easy to drop by to see her—she only lived around the corner—so a visit to Sarah could be squeezed into even the busiest day. I went over with the small cake and got the full treatment.

"O Lynn-dear, you remembered me, and how you do it I'll never know, and your husband is so lucky to have you with your curly hair and three children. Oh, what a miserable dog I am, to have no children—what a curse. Is this all—did you bring me a few little cans? Not that I'd expect anything, of course. . . ."

Sarah eventually got through to the core of my being—my prayer life. I could neither deal with her nor leave her alone. Some of the things that might be more appropriate to some of our people, especially those who came for Bible class or worship, would not be proper to discuss with Sarah. I did not know how to care for her. She was very needy, but required greater skill than I had, and I did not know how to help or how to be detached. I felt a sense of real failure, so I put her name on my prayer list for a while, hoping for inspiration. It also seemed that the spiritual element of her life was an unaddressed area, but I did not know how to do that either.

On a Tuesday, a usual visiting day, I was gathering a list of people to see, and Sarah's name popped into my head. A very strong sense that I should visit her accompanied this thought, plus the idea of going over to her room and reading psalms to her. It seemed a sort of unusual notion. I would take no food with me, then there would be no problem of what the missing item was. Something was always missing.

Against my will I was being dragged to her place at the same time that I was eager to get there. It was an approach-avoidance conflict, but with a Bible under my arm and a strange sense about at least having an agenda, I went around the block and up the back stairs to her apartment.

I knocked and the sad little voice said, "Who is it? Who? I can't see." She opened the door and peered at me, grabbing my arm with both hands to pull me closer and squint at me, at the same time drawing me into the tiny entryway of her apartment. "O Lynn-dear, thank God you've come," she said, leading me to sit down. She was sort of half crying, a bit more than her usual manner, and I explained that I thought she might like to hear some psalms from the Bible. Crying a bit, she explained that she had just had a phone call that morning. Her sister in Michigan had died, and there was only one other alive now besides her, and she had felt so all alone—how did I know to come that day?

How indeed? Sarah and I continued our odd relationship over the years. Whenever visitors came to The Ministry to get the tour, see what we did, or walk through the neighborhood, I would take them to visit Sarah. She so loved the company that she turned herself inside out, actually entertained people. Once she did a dance for a group of teens who visited from a suburban church youth group.

In my last visits with Sarah I often took a volunteer or other staff person with me, to aid in the transition of caregivers and to acquaint her with someone else. She had a final request. "Lynn-dear, could you do something for me? I want a bath. Can you find someone to give me a bath?"

I knew just the person—wonderful Jackie, our super volunteer who was also a nurse. It did make me a bit curious, though, so I asked her how she managed now.

"I wash myself in parts," she said.

Charles

*W*hat a day! It was the twelfth of March. Though in Chicago that's still winter, today the temperature was in the 60s and the sky was bright and blue. The snow, which clung to chunks of broken pavement and huddled in hills where it had been piled up by snowplows in the last snowstorm, was rotten, spongy-looking, and dirty, and there were puddles of water around. There would be more snow—winter was not over in this city—but the promise of spring was in the air and winter had lost its firm grip.

I looked out the window to see Charles walking toward the building. The sun glinted off the blue highlights in his dark-black skin, sharpened the line of the crease in the trousers of his navy-blue pinstripe suit, and sought out the few silver hairs of his short Afro hairstyle and made them sparkle. He wore a tie with blue stripes, crisp against his white shirt, and a carnation with baby's breath in his lapel. What a fox! He had a spring in his step, but he looked nervous.

Today was Charles and Penny's wedding day. That would account for the nervousness, right? Well, not all of it. Rhonda had misplaced his wedding ring!

Penny and Charles had been around the block a couple of times. They were not kids. Each had had children by a previous spouse, and Penny and Charles had a child together. They had been living together for several years, and Rhonda, their precocious three-year-old, was the spitfire of the preschool. The family lived in a nice apartment down the street with a large assortment of various-age children—a real case of his, hers, and theirs. Charles had been sent ahead by Penny because today they were not coming in together. They were observing tradition. Charles would wait for his bride. That was no easy task, and he was pacing. Pacing and pacing. What would they do without the ring? How had this happened?

Charles and Penny had been very pleased because they had finished paying off the rings that they had purchased on layaway. They would be wearing rings that were paid for—a source of pride. In the morning they had been showing these to folks, and Penny had been showing her dress, and people were running around preparing food; the household had been very chaotic. Rhonda had asked to see the ring, and the next anyone knew the ring was gone. The widow sweeping her house for the lost coin was a lesson in calm compared to the frenzy that hit the household. They went into high gear, secretly believing that Rhonda (who had a thing about being the center of the universe) had hidden it, and they were trying to coax clues out of her without alarming her and having her go into a sulk. No dice. They sifted through all the garbage in the house, worried that the ring had been flushed down the toilet, and checked and doublechecked every surface, crack, and crevice—all to no avail.

Although The Ministry was usually closed on Saturday, the whole staff was showing up for this grand event. Weddings were very rare at The Ministry, and this was to be a wedding with all the works. Penny had even requested "Here Comes the Bride." We still had a pastoral vacancy, which meant that we had visiting clergy to do services. The pastor was from a local parish that supported our work, and he had done the premarital counseling with the couple and was coming to perform the wedding ceremony. I had never met him.

I was scheduled to lead worship the next day and thought that perhaps I had a solution to Charles's problem. With a pastoral vacancy, the staff rotated worship, and I had been delighted to find that the lesson appointed for my day was the story of the prodigal son. The story ends with the statement, "Put a ring on his hand, and shoes on his feet; . . . for this my son was dead, and is alive again; he was lost, and is found" (Luke 15:22–24). I felt exceedingly self-satisfied because I had a cute idea: I'd gone to a children's party store and had purchased a bagful of ten-cent toy rings—party favors, really—and at that point of the parable planned to pass around the bag for people in the worshiping community to pick a ring. In school this would be called a visual aid. It was mildly dramatic, sweet, and friendly; the people would enjoy it, but they would also be feeling something tangible. As the jargon had it, "It worked for me."

"Charles, I think I have the solution!" I ran upstairs to my office and fetched the small brown-paper bag from my desk, and taking the stairs by twos, smugly presented the bag to Charles. He poured the rings out on the table—about thirty of the wildest, gaudiest creations imaginable, sure to delight six-year-olds—and tried them one by one. They didn't even come to the first knuckle. Charles had the largest fingers I had ever seen, and there was no way he was going to get married with any of these rings. Nice try, but no luck. "Don't worry, Charles, I know there's something in this building that will work."

I put the bag into the pocket of my suit, for I too was dressed up for the wedding, and began slowly to take in the details of the building. Curtain rings? Nope, there were only hooks. Kitchen drawers. Good idea! What's in here? Root, root, rummage, rummage. I pushed things aside, disturbed a few cockroaches, looked in the refrigerator, checked the back porch, went into the Learning Center and checked the stacks of boxes of supplies, then went upstairs to the offices. I walked around, looking up, then at eye level, then down, opened closet doors and squinted. I had no idea what I was looking for, but there had to be something. I paced and paced. I surveyed the bathroom. Nothing. I opened and closed desk drawers, mine and everyone else's, certain that there'd be that oddball item next to the paper clips. Nothing. I chewed on my lower lip, rubbed my chin, and absently pulled the tiny brown-paper bag out of my pocket to return it to my desk. My other hand rested idly by my suit jacket, and my eyes lit up. Keys! I carried a mess of keys—odd, because I rarely locked anything, even my house, but there were all these keys. There were car keys, office keys, house keys, desk keys, keys to friends' houses, the garage, the food pantry, the Learning Center. This wad of keys was loosely assembled onto four key rings, since people kept giving me key rings for gifts, and it was important to use things that people had chosen to give.

I ran downstairs. "Charles!" I called. "Come see! Try these. Does anything fit?" Charles tried the first one. Too small. "Hold on, there's another here someplace, there are two sizes. Maybe it's larger."

Charles grinned. "Well, I'll be." It was a fit.

Charles had come by the front door, from the sidewalk on Lakeside, but now there was sound in the back of the building. It was Penny and her entourage, arriving by the back door, having come through the alley. People began to assemble in the living room and dining area. I went to the kitchen to greet Penny, and she was nervous and funny. She wore a gorgeous blue lace dress, had delicate flowers in her curly black hair, and to keep from wrinkling herself had her sister bending over buckling her sandals. I complimented her on how lovely she looked, and she was quick to point out the price tag that was itching her where she'd carefully tucked it back inside her dress, up the sleeve under her arm. "First thing Monday I'm taking this back! I won't need it again, and it's too expensive to keep!" Everyone was laughing at Penny. Ever the practical mother of a large family, it was amazing that she was indulging herself in this much frill and frivolity.

The wedding was very lovely. There was music; Dorothy, one of our former staff people, had returned to sing a solo. With the vows there was a double-ring ceremony after all. When the service was over, we all accompanied the newlyweds to their apartment for a huge spread and a jolly reception. Some of the guests were mildly surprised that the staff people joined them, and we enjoyed giving the surprise. It was compounded by accepting a bottle of beer, visiting with the family, swapping small talk and lots of comments about the unseasonable weather. At some point in the afternoon, when Penny had drunk a toast or two, she was dancing cheek to cheek with Charles and wandered near her sister and asked to have her price tag cut off. She was going to keep the dress.

Cook County Hospital

On frequent occasions an "uncouple," Louise and Paul, came to the pantry. They were an uncouple in terms of marriage or an intimate relationship, but they were friends of long standing and shared an apartment.

Paul was a laconic kind of guy—he was friendly, could be chatty, but did not really give what could be called information or a history. In his early forties, he had pale blue eyes, one of which looked at you while the other did not. He was slender and tall, had thinning straight hair of a nondescript color, and a sallow complexion. His story was that at one time he had owned a chicken business, but either the business had failed, or his partner had left, or the city rent had caused him to lose the business, or it was a rented building that was sold and demolished. He supported himself by work through the day-labor agencies. My suspicions were that he drank—he had the signs of a heavy drinker—but that discussion would be put off for a while.

They rarely came to The Ministry together. Louise might come when things were rough and Paul was at the labor agency trying for a ticket. Paul might come if Louise was sick or if he had been unsuccessful getting a day's work he would stop by our pantry before going home again. Once in a while they came together, but only Louise would come upstairs; Paul would visit with other community people and drink coffee while waiting downstairs. It seemed almost circumspect.

Louise was much more informative. She was in her late fifties. She was a widow and told me about her husband, his death, and how she would pray, thanking God for the life she had had with her husband. Her husband had been sterile, the result of fever from malaria. He had been in the service for five years, serving for the full duration of World War II. Louise had never had children, but she had cared for her in-laws. Her husband developed diabetes and grew bitter. She received no general assistance, merely a small widow's pension. She was meek and warm and always had a smile. Except for Paul, she was alone. She had known Paul for years and was mildly critical of his ex-wife. Louise was protective of Paul. He did not speak of his divorce, but Louise did. She seemed like a big sister to him, almost motherly.

Louise had had a bout with cancer and said that she thanked God for each day she had. This gentle woman would sit and smile and talk softly about her faith, and I always felt as if I had been blessed after a visit with her—she was the Christlike servant, and I sat before her to learn.

Physically Louise looked run-down. She walked slowly, wore brown oxford shoes and had one crooked foot. She was of average height and build and had a nice face, unwrinkled, but the flesh seemed a bit shrunken under her skin. Her hair was the standout and startling part of her: she wore a wig. It was not the fact of wearing a wig that was startling: it was the wig she wore. It did not look like hair, but like a bath mat or like those fuzzy slippers that are supposed to look like moose or bears or some wild creature. It was like a brownish red rug on her head. She wore it like a hat. Trying not to look at Louise's head was an exercise in self-restraint. That effort to focus on something other than the top of her head forced me to look attentively at her eyes, which were lovely and invited me into her sweetness.

One day, on a slow food morning toward the beginning of the month, Paul called to say Louise wanted to speak to me. When she came on the phone she asked for prayers. She was frightened. She said she couldn't walk. I told her I'd be over that afternoon. Jackie was helping with food today—maybe she could come too.

I cleared that with Jackie and set about packing up a parcel for two people.

Louise lived about six blocks north, so we put the groceries in Jackie's car and left the office a bit early. Her building was difficult to get into, and if she could not get up to buzz us in, we would have to try other doorbells or hope that someone was coming out. It was a sunny afternoon on a cold, late-March day, and we got out of the car and rang the bell. Someone was coming out, so we slipped in the door and headed for the staircase. The sheet on file in the office indicated a second-floor apartment, so we began the climb. I had not been in this apartment building before.

Paul met us at the door. He was drunk, but with sufficient awareness of who we were to try desperately to pretend that he was in control. Poor man. He was weaving around, opening his eyes wide to try to focus his attention and reaching out for the door frame to attempt to steady himself, at which task he failed miserably. We smiled, handed him the groceries, and asked after Louise. She called from the living room, and we followed Paul through the apartment. He put the groceries in the small kitchen to the right, passing a small bedroom with a single mattress on the floor. The kitchen counter was empty of food, but there were a few empty beer cans around, and we averted our eyes on the way to the "front room," the universal expression in Uptown for living room.

I could sense Jackie's gasp as I inadvertently drew in my breath. The room was dark—there were curtains pulled across the windows, the TV was on, and Louise half sat, half sprawled across the cushion on the floor, her back propped against the couch. Her colostomy bag was leaking. She wore her hat/wig and a brown imitation-fur coat. The smell was worse than any barn I had ever been in, and the cigarette smoke probably enhanced rather than obscured the smell of human excrement and disease, stale beer, and an old TV dinner.

The situation was a new brick to be added to the pile of bricks that were labeled *"This is really the worst I have ever seen."* We were on our knees in a flash, and Louise relaxed with the relief of having been discovered and no longer having to keep up a pretense. She began to cry gently, and we put Paul to emptying the grocery bag to keep him out of the way. He was trying to talk and be helpful and was tripping over things, and it was impossible to listen to Louise.

Louise had fallen two days before and had not moved from the spot since. Jackie's educated guess was a broken hip. Having her here as a nurse was great because she would know what to do. Louise did not have a Medicaid card, locally called a green card. She was definite about not being able to go to the local hospital because of that. We called the local ambulance to check on that and were told that she was correct. They could transport her to the nearest hospital, which would verify that she received no Medicaid. Then she would be transferred to the county hospital. That procedure would take about three hours and she would be billed for the ambulance. We asked what to do, and they told us that the only option for the uninsured was the county hospital, which meant Chicago Cook County Hospital, on the South Side. As people said, "You have to go to the County."

Louise did not want to go, did not want to leave. Yet she also knew she needed help—it was obvious that Paul was useless to help her. She had a circle of things around her—cigarettes, pillows, a blanket, a coffee cup, the TV, a phone in her lap, and the remains of some sort of meal. Paul kept trying to reassure her that she was fine and continued to trip over things. This was a bad scene.

After thirty minutes of effort we convinced Louise of her need to be out of there and made the call to the ambulance people to assist. We alternated watching at the window with encouraging Louise that she was doing the best thing, and with attempting to convince Paul of Louise's need for help. The ambulance arrived shortly, and the attendants came in with a gurney to transport Louise down the stairs. The arrival of the ambulance brought the crowds out in full, and each window on the block and in the building framed a curious face. The crew carried her down as she patted Paul the way a knowing mother will pat a frightened child, while he made protestations about how she did not really need to leave— she could get better if she just rested.

The paramedics gently organized Louise's assortment of parts— hanging leg, enormous coat, slipping wig, and purse—into the back of Jackie's station wagon. We got in front and Jackie started up the engine. It was cold, a time for rolled-up windows and the heater, but the smell was so overpowering that we had to ride with windows open a little.

At this point we began to earnestly pray for a broken hip. If this woman had an injury that was incapacitating but did not require hospitalization, how could we ever return her to that mess? She would not get well if she was helpless and had to rely on Paul to care for her.

Jackie pulled up in front of the hospital emergency entrance and we were met by an attendant who scurried off to fetch a wheel-chair. Getting Louise out of the back seat and into the chair was no small engineering problem: she did not bend the way the car door hung. It took some time, but we managed. Jackie parked the car and met me at the front desk.

The hospital was huge. It seemed to stretch out everywhere. This was no modern building of sleek design, with wide-open curving and sweeping desks and corridors and furniture. The halls had pale walls of glazed tiles halfway up, angled intersections with high ceilings and narrow corridors, gray marbled floors with the brass separators between blocks, and they buzzed with many languages and dialects. There were very few white people around, and the impact of being a highly visible minority settled weightily on our shoulders.

We checked Louise in at the front desk. No modern, low-counter affair with a cutout for patient-receptionist dialogue, this affair had been built before the days of patient-rights regulations and handicap-access petitions. We served as interpreters between the receptionist, who sat at a high stool at a desk behind an elbow-level partition, and Louise, whose head was several inches lower, as she sat mercifully embraced by a wheelchair. To the question about religious affiliation, Louise sang out "Lutheran," and a smile escaped me. Louise was claiming identity.

For all that "going to the County" is spoken of in tones that one might use to speak of getting the plague, to a person, everyone we met was extraordinarily kind. These were sharp people, used to dealing with every problem under the sun, in triplicate and multi-lingually. We were given papers and assigned seats in a line of people waiting to be seen, who were a processional of medical problems. We took our place.

Everything was here: There were people standing with crutches, people holding other people, wheelchairs, gurneys, IV poles attached to stretchers and wheelchairs, people sitting with huge envelopes containing X-rays, someone with a gunshot wound, street drunks yellowed with jaundice, last-stage cancer patients with deep black circles under their eyes and no hair, and someone who was suspected of having had a heart attack. The smell that issued up from Louise's wheelchair was so repulsive that people would give a start at first, aghast, then give a wide berth as they walked by. Poor woman, she just sat with her head hung.

Jackie and I took turns going to the phone to call and let our families know where we were. I got through on the first try. Everyone was okay, but our son Andrew had dented a neighbor's new car. Wonderful! Jackie was having trouble. She had three daughters who were now between seventeen and twenty-three, and she was having a difficult time getting through. Her family often expected or at least allowed for the possibility of her being home very late on her Uptown volunteer day, but this day was going to be *very* late.

It was finally Louise's turn to be seen, and we took our places in the waiting room. Jackie continued to try the phone. It was now after seven, and we had left the office about three. We were here for the long haul and were just settling in to wait. The people in the waiting room were giving us the eye. Their inspection made us feel paler if anything, and Jackie seemed more blond than usual.

"You girls aren't from aroun' here, are you?"

"No, we brought somebody here."

"H-m, I though' so—sez to my frien' here, 'Those girls look lak thay's from upTOWN.'" When these women said *Uptown,* they were making a class distinction.

"Yes, you're correct. We do live on the North Side."

"How long you ladies been waitin' here?"

"We got here about four o'clock. How about you?"

"Oh, I be heah since 'bout one, my frien' heah since 'bout 'leven, but them peoples ovuh theah been heah since ten this mornin.'"

"It's really busy, isn't it? It is hard to wait so long, especially when you're sick. The lady we brought with us was in a lot of pain. That's probably why it was a bit quicker."

"Yas, I do believe you' right."

This was all pleasant and mild conversation, the invitation to talk extended by the "home team."

Our names were called about nine, and we were ushered back into the cavernous parts of the building to a room were Louise was on a stretcher, waiting. She still did not know if she was going to be admitted. The doctors in attendance were discussing this following the examination and would be in with their diagnosis and decision in a bit.

Louise had been X-rayed and bathed. She was wearing a clean blue-and-white johnny, her wig was off, revealing some fine, sparse, reddish hair. She was spanking-clean, and her skin had a little color and was shiny. She was thin with all of her layers of clothing removed, but was so clean she looked fantastic, though with such a different hairline, like an entirely different person.

Jackie asked permission to look at her middle, and Louise nodded, feeling quite comfortable with being handled at this point, and realizing that Jackie was a nurse. Jackie lifted the johnny gingerly and dissolved into tears.

"Oh, Louise, you haven't been taking care of yourself!"

Louise, after all this holding it together, now weakened herself and began to weep softly.

"I know," she whispered.

The cancer that Louise had had was colon cancer. She had had a colostomy, but she could not afford the cost of the bags. She had tried to reuse the bags, and the spillage of all that waste over a period of time had eaten a huge raw patch over her abdomen, which now looked like a large piece of raw meat. She hadn't been eating right and had bedsores and skin breakdown. Jackie looked up at me and mouthed inaudibly, "That's malnutrition." We stood on either side of her, holding her hands and awaiting the doctors as we patted and reassured her, giving each other the eye across Louise's middle—the silent prayer that she could stay here for care.

The doctors came in, confirmed for the three of us that Louise's hip was indeed broken and that they were admitting her to the ward. We kissed her good-bye, said our evening benediction and thanks to God at the same time, and walked to the door.

Jackie was parked on the street about three blocks away. The attendant looked at us, inquired of Jackie as to the whereabouts of her car, and allowed as how it was not safe for us to be out in this neighborhood at night. It was 10:30 P.M. He walked us to the car, tipped his hat, blessing us on our way. We did feel blessed on our way, safe in the suburban vehicle, with Louise safely tucked into a clean bed in this enormous old womb that cared for the city's poor.

Trinity

*W*e had been having problems with a guy named Joe who had been staying in the local shelter. Mental-health patients like Joe, living in the community without medication and perhaps on other drugs, were a danger to themselves, to our people, and to us. How did we care for these people? What was the best approach? One morning he had come in for food and was denied. He had come back again around noon. He seemed dangerous, and staff and other community people were afraid of him. It was not good to have someone around who terrorized people. Last week Mary Kay had been afraid to put him out because he seemed dangerous.

Marianka Fousek, pastor and our liaison to nursing homes, had told us about some very upsetting circumstances during worship the previous Sunday. Joe had been there, and so had Clayton, one of the people Mary Kay had been counseling, who she said was homicidal. Joe was black, and during the service Clayton began to make antiblack remarks. Joe went into the bathroom and began laughing hysterically. Marianka had been very frightened and did not know what to do.

This kind of problem did not happen very often, but when it did, it was scary. When Reverend Mick and Reverend Tom, both strong young men, had been around, and later Smitty, a tough older man, and Reverend Jim, an authoritative and calm man, there were others to turn to. Now, Mick and Tom were gone, Reverend Jim had had a stroke, and Smitty had died suddenly the previous summer. If Richard were out on a delivery or picking up groceries from a church, it was women only.

This afternoon the building had become very quiet. Roberta, Mary Kay, and Marianka had gone out to make home visits, it was Martha's day off, and Richard was out on errands. The afternoon lull of Ann doing paperwork at her desk in her office, Liz answering an infrequent phone call or pushing the carpet sweeper with its gentle click-click noise, was soothing. So soothing that I thought I had better fix a cup of tea before I fell asleep over my desk.

I stretched my arms and neck and walked down to the kitchen. The door into the pantry was ajar, letting in the cold air from the back porch. As I walked over to close it, noises from downstairs in the Learning Center area came to my ears, and I froze. It was not a Learning Center day—nothing was going on down there, and the Learning Center people were doing other things.

"Who's down there?" I called.

A voice said, "Joe."

I looked around for something to defend myself—a broom, a dustpan, rubber bands, anything! Very cautiously, I walked down the stairs, carefully leaving myself plenty of distance. As I peeked around the bottom of the stairs, visible under the basement hallway light was Joe Polk, a Native American community staff person, who was preparing to vacuum the Learning Center. A heavy sigh of relief escaped, and I walked over and explained my fright to Joe.

Deadpan, he said, "I should have said, 'Indian Joe.'"

I went back to my desk, pulled out the bottom drawer, put my feet up, and one by one took the charts from the pile stacked on my desk and read over the notes from the morning's interviews. Arne, who now participated in food interviews as well as being business manager, had had a tough one.

Arne's joining the staff had been a great relief. He had been the treasurer on our board for some time, and following Smitty's death we had been desperate for a business manager. Arne's favorite snack food was potato chips, so for his welcoming lunch each of us had brought a bag of potato chips in a different flavor. The jolliness said a lot about the flavor of the staff.

When I had pulled the chart for Countess from the stack of interviews, I had decided to put it back and leave it for someone else. A new staff person might have a new view of things.

Countess lived across the street, and was an A-number-one pain. She was pushy, demanding, irritating, and would not shut up. She and her husband lived in a low-rent building, but she always demanded food for about eight, insisting that she fed all her grandchildren. I reacted to her with the worst in me. Now I opened the file, recognized Arne's handwriting, and expecting paragraphs of comments was disappointed to find only a few words—until I read them: "Old Deep South talking to 'the Man.'" A new staff person had a new perspective, all right, Were we lucky!

Nathan showed up, and I took him up to my office to show him Vermont pictures. I had a huge state map on the office door, and a few pictures clipped on top to give people an idea of where I and my family were moving and to share some of that with them. While Nathan was looking at the map and pictures, I found the new letter of reference and got it all ready for him. He checked the letter over, said it was OK, and we chatted a bit about Vermont and life. "That's the closest thing on earth to heaven, Vermont, the country. . . . As you grow older, you gain grace and wisdom. . . ." What a likable man, this Nathan.

We walked into the backyard so I could take his picture. I had one photo of the two of us taken a few summers ago, but today he really looked like a dude. He was wearing a three-piece gray pinstripe suit, a white shirt, and a necktie. Black was not only beautiful, this black man was dignified and whole.

Trinity Sunday was coming in two weeks and we needed a banner, so after a trip to the fabric store, another banner had appeared in the rear living room. Again, people sought out the needles and thread and took up the stitching.

Mary Kay had agreed to do the homily for church because Trinity Sunday was a very special day to her. The banner was almost finished, and Pam and Penny had said they would come to work on it Thursday morning while their children attended the preschool time. Pam and Russell, like Penny and Charles, had been married at The Ministry. I was clearing a few things off my desk when there was a huge commotion down in the kitchen—shrieking and laughing and squealing and carrying on—and I stopped what I was doing to listen and to try to make sense out of some of the words. Penny's voice emerged from the noise. When I heard the word "ring" I was out of my chair and down the stairs two at a time.

Penny was laughing and smiling. They had found Charles's wedding ring. When she had been putting away winter clothes, she pulled a suit hanger from the closet—one with a broad hanger for the jacket and a pants hanger attached with a loop over the hook of the jacket hanger. As she had lifted the pants hanger to put away a winter suit, there over the hook was Charles's wedding ring.

Roberta walked with me to the elevated train that afternoon. A young, enthusiastic art teacher, she had brought unique additions to the staff and especially the preschool program. I had a wall filled with pictures of community people, family, and staff, so I took a photograph of Roberta standing in front of a car advertising the fried-chicken place at the corner. The car, white on the bottom, had the top half in the shape of a giant hen! The picture would remind me of her special contribution to The Ministry.

On Sunday, the living room had been rearranged for worship, the hymnals in place, the candles, cross, and altar linens arranged, bulletins on the chairs, and banner hung. People began to arrive and greet Mary Kay, and I went to the piano to play the hymns. It was a lovely service, and Mary Kay spoke beautifully. Almost everyone had gone when I glanced up at the banner and realized that it was hanging upside down.

"Mary Kay, look," I moaned. "The banner, I don't believe it—I hung it upside down!"

Her eyebrows went up and she chuckled. "That's part of the mystery of the Trinity!"

John

*M*ary Kay and I went back to the office late one afternoon following a particularly sad mission—the funeral and burial of a four-day-old infant who had died from a severe heart defect. The crowd had dispersed in clumps of denim-clad youth and confused extended family members and neighbors. Mary Kay and I, now apart from the family talk, drove the eight blocks north to the office.

The building was eerily quiet and felt beige. It had the slanting mellow daylight of late afternoon sun, somewhat obscured by the tall buildings all around and the trees in our yard. It was after office hours, locked up tight, no people, no piles of stuff around, no noise, no phones, no bustle. It was stark still. In a busy, noisy city, in a part of the city full of high-rise tenement apartments teeming with kids and the noise of ambulances, police cars, and fire engines, the quiet of this three-story brick house with the two-foot-deep walls was a paradox. One could walk in and be in another world.

We made small talk about the funeral. The family seemed to be taking this well. Will Bradley and Kim stay together, do you think? The undertaker was kind, wasn't he? I never saw such a small casket. . . .

Upstairs I stuffed the leftover bulletins in my desk, set down my purse, and called home to tell whoever answered that I was still in the city but would be on my way home shortly. Dinner might be a little late, but not much, and how was your day, and yes, mine too, and I'll tell you all about it when I get home. Love you too. First I'll check my desk for messages. None. Pick up the mail—Uh-oh.

My arms began to tingle with the odd numb feeling, and anxiety occupied my stomach. Nausea. "Mary Kay, look at this."

Carrying the envelope, with my eyes trying to focus, I walked into May Kay's office. I held the envelope in front of her. She adjusted her glasses, then looked up at me over the black rims. "What do you think?"

"Nothing good," I said, carrying it back to my desk. It was a letter-sized envelope, one of our own, with a drawing of our building on it. I knew—I'd drawn it. It was my handwriting, my name in the upper left-hand corner, and it was addressed to John. There was the large purple hand with pointing finger stamped on by the U.S. Post Office, which read, "Returned to sender—attempted—not known." In poorly formed, handwritten capital letters printed over the address it said, "NOT AT—DIED."

I walked into the large front office where the files were. Though there was still plenty of light at five o'clock in the afternoon in June, this northeast room, sunny and warm in the morning, was heavily shadowed now. The walls were soft turquoise, there was a large fireplace with oak mantel that matched the doors and woodwork all around the room, and extended above the mantel was fancy carved wood with an oval mirror set in. It was a cozy spot that seemed secure and woodsy. I did not bother with the light, but pulled open the file drawer of the equally old and heavy oak filing cabinet. I pulled out John's file and took it over to the desk by the windows. Riffling through the pages, I found some entries about when John had last been around. February was the last, although there was a note that Sister Mary Kay had seen him during Holy Week, very drunk, swearing and shouting obscenities at the group of worshipers who were walking the stations of the cross in the neighborhood. The note said that he looked very thin and sick. I closed my eyes, exhaled some, and turned to the back inside cover of the manila folder. It was covered with a long list of names and phone numbers that included hospitals, hospital social workers, priests, and the nursing home where John had lived, plus their social service worker, head nurse, doctor, and so on. There were also family members: John's brother-in-law on the North Side, and John's twin, Jane. I wrote her number on the back of the returned envelope, replaced the file in the cabinet, closed the heavy drawer with my shoulder, and went back to my office, where I put the envelope and phone number in my pocketbook.

"Mary Kay, I'll call you if I find out anything."

"Please do, Lynn—I'll be home."

Now I was weary—really weary. This was a call I could hardly wait to make yet did not want to make at all. It was five thirty when I got home, still too early to call someone who would have an hour's commute. I'd wait until after supper. I chatted with the kids, asked Bon about the time of the soccer picnic and awards evening, chatted with Andrew about his day, and patted the dogs as they ran in circles wagging their whole bodies for attention. Scott came down from his office to inquire about my day and give me a hug. I showed him the envelope. He raised his eyebrows, but I just shook my head.

"I'm going to call John's twin sister, Jane, after supper."

We ate in a semihaze for me—I was distracted and eager for the time to tick by, anticipating what Jane would say. Finally—half past seven. This is enough time—she'll have gotten home, eaten, organized herself. Get out the buried envelope, dial the phone.

"Hello?"

"Hi, this is Lynn Perry from The Ministry. Is this Jane?"

"Just a minute, I'll get her. Hey, Mom? For you."

"Hello?"

"Hi, Jane, this is Lynn Perry from The Ministry. I'm calling to ask you about John. I sent him a letter that was returned today in the mail, and I wanted to call you to ask about him."

"Who did you say this is?"

"I'm Lynn Perry. I work at The Ministry, and John used to come to us to get food. You came to talk to me about John when—"

"Oh, yeah, I remember now. Right. Well, Jack died of cancer last month. We had the funeral two weeks ago, and he was buried in the family plot in St. Stephen's Cemetery."

I made some weak condolence remarks. Jane seemed relieved that the ordeal and saga of her wayward twin was finally over with, and that was that.

And when the wind starts to howl on a cool gray night, it's somebody crying for John this night, someone who knew old John when he wasn't old—when he wasn't hungry and he wasn't cold. Someone who knew old John when he was going on sixteen. He was just as good as anyone. Going on sixteen he was danger's darling, he was fortune's favorite son. Laughter followed him around. Brighter than the sun were his eyes, ablaze with the fire of youth, that only the darkness could dim. . . . But he's dead now, and the wind mourns alone. . . . [1]

The haunting melody from the Gordon Jenkins reverie began to play itself in my head, the words and melody rolling slowly by to salute old John. Now I really was tired. I could taste the salt in the back of my mouth and feel the hot tears on my face. God, I was weary. I picked up the phone and dialed a city number again. Mary Kay answered, and I told her that John was dead.

"Oh, no," she said softly. "But I'm not surprised, really—he was looking rough the last time I saw him on the street. Are you all right?"

I said that no, I wasn't, but there wasn't anything to be done about it. I said good night and hung up. My crew had gone out to catch the last of the fading daylight in a little neighborhood Frisbee game. The house was quiet before the onslaught of the players who'd soon come crashing in for a cold drink and dessert.

Sitting on the kitchen stool by the phone, I opened my purse to return John's letter with the phone number on the back. Instead of putting it back, though, I held it in my hand, staring at the address and remembering. I had worked hard to compose it—to try to strike the perfect balance. It was still fresh in my mind:

Dear John,

It's been a long time since you've stopped by The Ministry, and in case you had no plans to visit, I wanted to give you some information. This summer our family is moving to Vermont. My last day at the office will be July 21. I will try to stop by some day before that for a visit, but in case I don't get to it, I did not want to leave town without saying good-bye to you. Although I haven't seen you, other staff people have. They say that you look quite thin and at times have looked very angry. That saddens me. I keep hoping that one of these days you'll choose life and health. If you and I don't cross paths before I leave, I want you to know that I've enjoyed having you for a friend and will always remember you.

Peace, Lynn Perry

I sat for a while, quietly, just holding the letter. I wonder if John knew that I loved him? I hoped so.

1. Gordon Jenkins, "The Caretaker," *Seven Dreams,* ©1953 Decca Records, Inc., DL 9011.

Oreste

It seemed as if I was just going through the motions the following Monday, and so I was stunned to find a sweet basket on my desk the next morning, filled with spring flowers. The note read, "Dear Lynn, I wish this had more daisies for you! I wish I could say, as beautifully as these flowers, how sorry I am about John, how happy I am you have a new home in a lovely spot, and how much I care about you. Peace to you always! Love, Ann."

Our daughter Amy was getting married, and we would be moving to Vermont. I would miss this loving and compassionate staff, with dear friends like Ann.

It was a crowded food morning, and with thirty people in for food and three of us interviewing, it was noisy, crowded, and busy. Listening, trying to understand, to be attentive, and to give compassionate help was hard, stressful work.

Leonard was in my office, and we were having a bit of a hard time getting down to cases. The word was that Leonard had been drinking pretty heavily, and while it was easy to deny food to someone who smelled of alcohol, hearsay was not a reason to deny food. Asking questions about why food stamps had lasted only one week was more the approach.

My desk was long, and it faced the wall, with a drawer in the center, drawers on the side, and a pullout writing surface above the drawers. When someone was in the office to talk, I liked to pull the writing surface out and sit on the other side of it, with the person's file on it, then have the visitor sit in the comfortable chair. That way we sat face to face; it was a friendlier, less institutional posture for both of us.

Leonard sat opposite me, his long, lanky legs crossed at the calf, and prepared to lecture me about living on the street. I was ready to challenge him about his need for food and what he had been doing with his money. As he talked about some of the things he wanted to eat, I squinted a bit and pointedly asked him how, considering he had no teeth, he proposed to eat some of the things he was talking about.

"Lady, I go behind the Wilton House. They feed them old peoples pretty good over there, and them peoples don' eat a halft o' what's given 'em. There be's pretty good garbage behind there. I gets me a box an' goes ovah behint the place and takes the chicken, and then I takes it home and washes it all off and takes off the skin and fries up a bit o' margarine and cooks that chicken, and it nice and tender. Don' need no teeth for that. One day me an' Bill was behind back there pickin' through the garbage when this ole man comes along and starts in going through the stuff hisself, and I tole him to get away, and when he didn' I hits him with a stick an' says, 'Ole man, you gets yo'sef yo' own box! This is my garbage!'"

I just shook my head and wrote out the familiar slip of paper—food for one, LP—and handed it to Leonard to take downstairs to Richard. No sense putting any special dietary requests on it. If Leonard was eating garbage, I guessed he would make do.

We were about halfway through the list, and it was about ten thirty. We should be finished about noon unless someone had a very serious problem that would take a long interview time. I pulled the next chart, read the previous entry and pertinent information, checked the green-card date, then walked down the stairs to call the next person on the list and escort the person to my room.

I checked the top information. Still at the same address? Still the same number of people in the household? How are you getting along? Then I started in on the "What-brings-you-here-today?" type of questions.

Halfway into our visit Liz buzzed me. I picked up the intercom line, and she told me that Terry was calling from the Convalescent Home. I excused myself and picked up the phone. Terry's call was to let me know that they had just called the ambulance for Oreste. He was having problems breathing, and she thought that I'd want to say good-bye to him before he went to the hospital. I thanked her and hung up. I cut the interview as short as possible, made certain that there were no outstanding problems, and offered, as always, the resources of Bible class, Learning Center, and worship, and the reminder that we were open all week and were available for any problems that might come up.

I popped my head into Mary Kay's office to tell her where I was headed and that I'd be right back, told the person on duty, and told Liz on the way down the stairs, which I took two at a time.

It was early February and cold. I must have been crazy not to stop for a coat, but I alternately jogged and walked fast, and it was only three blocks to the Convalescent Home.

The ambulance was already in front of the building, and they were wheeling Oreste out on a gurney. He looked so frail strapped onto that rig with blankets pulled tightly around him that I could readily see how wasted he had become. I stood there holding my arms, hopping from foot to foot to keep warm and staring at Oreste. He saw me, but was unable to say my name. I nodded and smiled, but he just stared back at me. His eyes didn't leave my face, and it seemed that if I turned away he would evaporate. I kept watching him and hopping, and he kept watching me but was too weak to speak.

Gloria lived across the street and hollered over, "Is that Oreste?" and it made me mad. Here was a poor dying man, and she was hollering at me across the street to find out who it was. I just stood there and didn't acknowledge the question, just pretended I didn't hear, and after a while Gloria went away.

"Come on here, guys, let's go," one of the attendants said.

"We can't leave until we get a line in," the other answered, and they worked on Oreste while he continued to stare at me.

"Look, we could have been to the hospital and back three times already—let's just go!"

"We can't. It's the regulation. We can't leave here until we have a needle in. If anything happened during transport, we would have to be able to run a line immediately. We have to have access to a vein."

I was aware that it had begun to snow, fat fluffy flakes, and I was cold on the outside and my stomach was in knots. What was the matter with me? This man was not a relative. So what if he called me his daughter, Lee. So what if he had even introduced me as his wife. He was just a mixed-up old man! What was I doing out here without a coat in the snow? Who was crazy?

It took half an hour, but they finally got a needle into Oreste and they were set. They anchored the gurney in the ambulance and shut the back doors. I peeked through the window and waved as the paramedics ran to the front, flung open the doors, and hopped inside. They put the ambulance into gear and headed north on Kenmore—"lights and sirens."

I stared after them, exhausted suddenly, and still cold but too depressed to jog. I walked back to the office.

The last really good visit with Oreste had been on his birthday, a month and a half before. He was always talking about wanting spaghetti, so I made a meatball and spaghetti dinner, and we had a staff lunch with Oreste. I asked him what kind of cake he wanted, and he said, "Vanilla," so vanilla it was. We took pictures, had a lot of laughs, and Oreste ate three helpings of spaghetti then sat around in the afternoon and visited, but he really looked as if he was failing. The fight was gone out of him, and this man would not be living independently ever again.

I saw Oreste at the hospital the next day, and he did not look good. The following week when I stopped by he was not in his room. He had been transferred to the coronary care unit. He appeared to be hooked to one of everything. He was clean, coherent, and peaceful.

A week later I stopped at the hospital again, and after waiting in the anteroom for admission to the coronary care unit, was told that Oreste had been returned to his previous room. He was a shocking sight, and he looked awful. He had a feeding tube and kept hollering, "Take it off, I want to sleep. Take it off, I want to sleep!" He had been carrying on for some time. He asked for his glasses, and I went to find a nurse. She was obviously annoyed and did not know anything about his glasses. When I returned to the room Oreste started to pull at the feeding tube. It made me nauseated, and I hollered for the nurse. A nurse and an aide came, and they were furious. Apparently it had been very difficult to insert the tube. I said I had tried to get help, and the nurse snapped, "You should have held his hands!" It had never even occurred to me. I looked at his hands—they were in restraints. I noticed again how he watched me but closed his eyes and looked away when I looked at him. He was refusing to eat and being very uncooperative. The nurses were really having problems with him. Poor lonely old man.

Oreste was back from the hospital for only about a month before Terry called again to say that they were returning him to the hospital. Again I ran over, but now it was April and warmer.

When I arrived, Oreste was being put into the ambulance, and this time he was on oxygen. As soon as he saw me he asked for a cigarette. I closed my eyes and shook my head: no matter how sick he was, he was Oreste!

Two weeks later Oreste was back at the Convalescent Home, and I began a day of visiting by stopping to see him. He was looking pretty good then.

In mid-May, returning from my daughter's soccer game about suppertime, I found an urgent message to call a city phone number that I did not recognize. I called, and a nurse told me that Oreste was being prepped for surgery; then the doctor came on the phone. Oreste had peritonitis from an old ulcer that had perforated.

"I'm not eager to operate on this man. He's old and his health is not good, but we must do the best by him, and without surgery he'll die."

I left the house and went to the hospital. I read the Twenty-third Psalm and held his hand.

"How's Sister Kay?" he asked, and, "Why doesn't she wear a uniform?" Mary Kay was fine, I assured him, and Franciscan sisters who worked in the community dressed like regular people.

"Why can't I live with you? You can have my whole check. I'll do my own cooking. Just give me a little money for cigarettes. Why didn't you come Tuesday and bring me ice cream?"

"What?" I said involuntarily, a bit muddled, and not quite knowing which question to answer first.

"What's the matter with you," he screamed at me. "Are you deaf? I'm afraid!"

Oreste pulled through the surgery and once again was back at the Convalescent Home. I brought ice cream bars when I visited. In early July I visited him for the last time. Oreste had a breathing tube and complained that it choked him. He was in restraints, was catheterized, and wearing diapers. As I got up to leave, I waved, and in an unlike-Oreste gesture he raised his mittened hand to wave back and said, "Bye-bye."

Worship

*T*his was my last week. Sister Mary Kay said I was in denial and I denied it, but she was right. Perhaps I was afraid of falling to pieces, or worse, that no one would care that I was leaving anyway, so I wrapped myself in a veneer of steely control and marched gingerly through the week. All the preparations for our daughter Amy's wedding would be fun, but first I had to get through this final week.

As coordinator for the staff, Mary Kay had suggested that I begin to eliminate regular duties two weeks before final termination, so I had ceased to do food interviews and was not responsible for a day on duty. There were many people to say good-bye to and, in the course of all the home visits I made, I passed many others on the street. It was always fun to be howdyed on the street—to feel that sense of community in this densely populated section of a large, major city.

I visited with Virginia, who was experiencing excruciating pain in her arms. She was unable to wash or dress herself, certainly not able to do any quilting, and was convinced that she was dying of cancer for misbehavior she had committed as a young child. I had visited Oreste,who was out of the hospital, intubated with an IV and a catheter. He was as thin as a rail and twice as frail. I saw Sarah again.

I could feel myself holding my body rigid and my thoughts aloof from the rest of the staff, but I seemed helpless to let loose. A church group from Wisconsin came in for a visit, and as my time was not scheduled, I toured them through the community with stops at local sites such as St. Thomas's, pointing out the Center for Street People and the Catholic Worker House and the REST Shelter.

Thursday was Jackie's workday, and she often drove me home.

She had a long drive north, and dropping me off broke up her trip and was marvelous door-to-door service for me.

We always talked a mile a minute, the drive went fast, and we would wind up talking in the driveway even longer. In the past months, most of that conversation had been about moving and wedding plans. Today's chat began as usual, but somewhere in the course of the conversation we began to talk of the changes we had seen in The Ministry over the years. Jackie said, "Of all the things I've seen change, and all the people, I think that the greatest change has taken place in Martha."

"What do you mean?"

"Well, when I first met Martha, she was so different, and now, here she is, a member of the staff—"

"When did you first meet Martha?"

"Oh, it was Christmas, many years ago, and Martha had been sick . . ."

"Yes," I said.

". . . and our children were helping friends from school whose church was doing stuff with The Ministry . . ."

"What?"

". . . They were gathering things for families, and we got the name of Martha and the children, and Richard . . ."

"You?"

". . . and we got a tree with decorations, and put together a turkey dinner . . ."

"You? You were the ones? You were the family that did all that stuff for Martha's family that year she and Richard had both been sick?"

"Well, yes."

"Does Martha know it was you—that you are the ones?"

"I don't know. It was a long time ago."

"And did you know, Jackie, that in all these years, when she goes places to speak, or when anybody asks her why she came here, she talks about that Christmas, and that wonderful family who came and brought presents for everyone, and a tree, and dinner, and how she came to volunteer at The Ministry after that, and about how it was the best Christmas her family had ever had?" I shrieked.

"No, I didn't know that," Jackie mused, quite subdued.

I thanked her for the ride, told her I'd see her at the farewell party the next week, and tore into the house. I let my bag and papers slide into a chair in the hall and headed for the phone.

"Hi, Martha—guess what I just learned?"

My last Sunday for worship arrived, and Sister Mary Kay had wanted to have a "do" of some sort—treats, coffee, and visiting time—but I had said no. I was self-conscious at parties, and this was no different. I was nervous enough about saying good-bye to staff and board members.

We still had a staff vacancy for a full-time pastor, and I was to lead worship. The lesson for the day was from Luke, the story of the good Samaritan. If I had had my choice to pick anything I wanted, I don't think I could have picked any better than the lesson appointed for that seventeenth day of July. I composed my homily and selected the hymns, all sentimental choices: "I Love to Tell the Story," "In the Garden," and "The Church's One Foundation."

Scott chose to come with me that last Sunday. He or one of the children came on occasion but usually had commitments at our own church, so this was a special offering to me. People began to filter in the front door as I was rearranging the room and setting up the worship area for the service. I greeted a person and went upstairs for the altar cloths, greeted someone else and went back up for the cross and candlesticks, set out hymnals, greeted another and went upstairs to get the bulletins, vases, and my Bible and homily—the good Samaritan, God's Samaritan.

When it came time to begin and I finally faced the group who had come, the makeup of the congregation startled me—good Samaritans, all. Arne, our business manager, and Mary Kay were there from the staff, which was not shocking, but Richard Grooms was there also, and that was. To the best of my knowledge Richard had never come to worship there before—I don't even think he came when his kids were baptized. It wasn't that Richard didn't believe in God, but he had had such a rigid and strict religious indoctrination in a very fundamentalist environment that he just could not do it. Yet here he was.

There would be endless stories to tell about Richard—his

warmth, his humor, his generosity. One day, sometime after his son, who had been hit by a car, was out of the hospital and out of danger, Richard brought me a poem he'd written for me because I'd come right down to the hospital to be with them. One day he walked into my office, came around behind me, then leaned over and gave me a kiss on the cheek, very shyly, turned beet-red, and said, "That's for something you did a long time ago, and it meant a lot to me, but I didn't realize how much at the time. Think about it," and he was gone. We talked later, and what he was referring to was a time when things were rough between him and Martha. I was visiting them in their apartment, and on the way out I had told Richard that I loved him as well as Martha. Richard's act of affection and affirmation that day was a special grace, for the next day I flew home to New York to be with my father, who was dying. And once when my husband was out of work, Richard had handed me an envelope with one hundred dollars in it. And here was Richard in church—the same, funny, Georgia-born-and-bred Richard who had said to Martha, "No matter how smart any woman is, doesn't matter if she's a doctor, has a Ph.D., or what, she's still not equal to any man, no matter how ignorant he is." Richard, what a fake. Loving and sincere, he may have thought he believed that, but his actions proved he didn't. And here it was Sunday, and here was Richard, by the grace of God, and by the grace of God I was allowed to be there too. I began to wonder if I was going to get through this morning without going to pieces.

Among the regulars present were Floyd, Reba, Lucille, and Arthur. He had moved farther north, but was driven in for worship, and he played the tambourine. Then there were the surprises: Mary Kay's roommate, Sister Patricia! Linda, our summer intern; Richard Walker; Hal; Charles, wearing his wedding ring; Leonard—I thought he was still in prison!—and Russell, one of the preschool dads. It was a large crowd, and it really pleased me, but seeing who composed the crowd awed me.

When I glanced over at Lucille, who was looking healthy today, I suppressed a chuckle thinking about the cats. Lucille loved animals, especially cats, and she took in strays. In fact, Lucille took in so many stray cats that Sister Mary Kay had an arrangement with some animal protection group to bring cat food to Lucille on a regular basis, in large economy quantities, so Lucille would not spend all her food money on cat food.

Once when Lucille was in the hospital, Ann was appointed the "cat feeder person" and returned from Lucille's apartment in shock: there were over twenty cats there! Something had to be done—it was hardly sanitary. Ann and Martha scooped up more than a dozen cats—there were still plenty left for Lucille—thinking that the humane society would take them. No way. There was a charge if they were to be put to sleep, and the agency refused to find homes for them unless the animals had all their shots and had been neutered. The request was reasonable, but impossible to fulfill.

So, late on a Thursday afternoon, long after the close of office hours, Ann and Martha were riding around the city with a carload of cats they could not unload. They drove more and more westerly, trying one place after the other, until they had reached the city limits. Emotionally out of gas, they pondered their plight. Martha got a glint in her eye, gestured with her head in the direction of a cemetery that had a stream running through it with large weeping willow trees lining the banks, branches draping, and said, "How about it, Ann? I've had enough for today. Whaddaya say we let 'em loose here?"

"Well, they'll probably just be stray cats that will wander back into the city, and Lucille will rescue them again," Ann moaned.

"Yeah, maybe so, but it'll take 'em a while. And you never know—it's nice and pleasant here, cool—maybe they'll fish and just be content to stay here."

And it was done—the liberation of the cats.

After the homily and the prayer time, I looked up at these good Samaritans, God's good Samaritans to me, and saw Mary Kay give me a "look." It was one of her special looks, one of those "You-may-think-you're-in-charge-but-there's-Someone-more-in-charge-than-you-and-other-forces-that-are-operative-here" looks, and she slipped out the back kitchen door with an impish smile on her face.

She was back before the close of the final hymn, bringing a large assortment of doughnuts, and the coffeepot was on. She explained, "Some refreshments so people can visit, Lynn."

The final sacramental meal.